THE INSPIRATIONAL
Christmas Almanac

HEART WARMING TRADITIONS,
TRIVIA, STORIES, AND RECIPES
FOR THE HOLIDAYS

RACINE, WI

The Inspirational Christmas Almanac

ISBN: 978-1-970103-61-8 - *Paperback*
ISBN: 978-1-970103-62-5 - *Hardcover*
ISBN: 978-1-970103-63-2 - *Ebook*

Copyright © 2022 by Honor Books
Racine, WI

Cover design by Faille Schmitz

Dear Reader

Congratulations. You hold in your hand The Inspirational Christmas Almanac. It is our sincere wish that this book will help make your Christmas both more fun and more meaningful to you and your family. We hope it will play a significant role in creating Christmas memories for many years.

The almanac can be used in one of two ways. First, you can close your eyes and open the book anywhere and jump right in. You'll find trivia, stories, carols, Scriptures, recipes, crafts, and other information to enhance your experience of Christmas in all its spectacular glory.

Or, if you prefer, you can start at the beginning and read straight through the book. We have arranged the book's sections in a logical flow that will help prepare your heart for the holiday, reflect on the depths of meaning in the season, find the joy and laughter of Christmas, and then shine the light of Christmas among your family, friends, and community with creative crafts, inspired recipes, and thoughtful service projects that can communicate the true meaning of this most meaningful of holidays.

You'll find the following sections in the almanac:

Inspirational Christmas Stories
Poems, Carols, and Readings
Reflections on the Meaning of Christmas
The True Story of Christmas

Our prayer for you is that *The Inspirational Christmas Almanac* will be a means by which the love and joy of Christ will pour over you and yours — both this Christmas and for many, many more Christmases to come.

Merry Christmas!

THE EDITORS

Contents

SECTION 1

Inspirational Christmas Stories

PAPA PANOV'S SPECIAL CHRISTMAS

LEO TOLSTOY

It was Christmas Eve and although it was still afternoon, lights had begun to appear in the shops and houses of the little Russian village, for the short winter day was nearly over. Excited children scurried indoors and now only muffled sounds of chatter and laughter escaped from closed shutters.

Old Papa Panov, the village shoemaker, stepped outside his shop to take one last look around. The sounds of happiness, the bright lights and the faint but delicious smells of Christmas cooking reminded him of past Christmas times when his wife had still been alive and his own children little. Now they had gone. His usually cheerful face, with the little laughter wrinkles behind the round steel spectacles, looked sad now. But he went back indoors with a firm step, put up the shutters and set a pot of coffee to heat on the charcoal stove. Then, with a sigh, he settled in his big armchair.

Papa Panov did not often read, but tonight he pulled down the big old family Bible and, slowly tracing the lines with one forefinger, he read again the Christmas story. He read how Mary and Joseph, tired by their journey to Bethlehem, found no room for them at the inn, so that Mary's little baby was born in the cowshed.

"Oh, dear, oh, dear!" exclaimed Papa Panov, "if only they had come here! I would have given them my bed and I could have covered the baby with my patchwork quilt to keep him warm."

He read on about the wise men who had come to see the baby Jesus, bringing him splendid gifts. Papa Panov's face fell. "I have no gift that I could give him," he thought sadly.

Then his face brightened. He put down the Bible, got up and stretched his long arms to the shelf high up in his little room. He took down a small, dusty box and opened it. Inside was a perfect pair of tiny leather shoes. Papa Panov smiled with satisfaction. Yes, they were as good as he had remembered — the best shoes he had ever made. "I should give him those," he decided, as he gently put them away and sat down again.

Best of all, Christmas means a spirit of love, a time when the love of God and the love of our fellow men should prevail over all hatred and bitterness, a time when our thoughts and deeds and the spirit of our lives manifest the presence of God.

GEORGE E MCDOUGALL

He was feeling tired now, and the further he read the sleepier he became. The print began to dance before his eyes so that he closed them, just for a minute. In no time at all Papa Panov was fast asleep.

And as he slept he dreamed.

He dreamed that someone was in his room and he knew at once, as one does in dreams, who the person was.

It was Jesus.

"You have been wishing that you could see me, Papa Panov," he said kindly, "then look for me tomorrow. It will be Christmas Day and I will visit you. But look carefully, for I shall not tell you who I am."

When at last Papa Panov awoke, the bells were ringing out and a thin light was filtering through the shutters. "Bless my soul!" said Papa Panov. "It's Christmas Day!" He stood up and stretched himself for he was rather stiff. Then his face filled with happiness as he remembered his dream. This would be a very special Christmas after all, for Jesus was coming to visit him. How would he look? Would he be a little baby, as at that first Christmas? Would he be a grown man, a carpenter — or the great King that he is, God's Son?

He must watch carefully the whole day through so that he recognized him however he came.

Papa Panov put on a special pot of coffee for his Christmas breakfast, took down the shutters and looked out of the window. The street was deserted, no one was stirring yet. No one except the road sweeper. He looked as miserable and dirty as ever, and well he might! Whoever wanted to work on Christmas Day — and in the raw cold and bitter freezing mist of such a morning?

FACTOID

Theodore Roosevelt, a staunch conservationist, banned Christmas trees in his home, even when he lived in the White House. His children, however, smuggled them into their bedrooms.

Papa Panov opened the shop door, letting in a thin stream of cold air. "Come in!" he shouted across the street cheerily. "Come in and have some hot coffee to keep out the cold!"

The sweeper looked up, scarcely able to believe his ears. He was only too glad to put down his broom and come into the warm room. His old clothes steamed gently in the heat of the stove and he clasped both red hands round the comforting warm mug as he drank.

Papa Panov watched him with satisfaction, but every now and then his eyes strayed to the window. It would never do to miss his special visitor.

"Expecting someone?" the sweeper asked at last. So Papa Panov told him about his dream.

"Well, I hope he comes," the sweeper said, "you've given me a bit of Christmas cheer I never expected to have. I'd say you deserve to have your dream come true." And he actually smiled.

When he had gone, Papa Panov put on cabbage soup for his dinner, then went to the door again, scanning the street. He saw no one. But he was mistaken. Someone was coming.

The girl walked so slowly and quietly, hugging the walls of shops and houses, that it was awhile before he noticed her. She looked very tired and she was carrying something. As she drew nearer he could see that it was a baby, wrapped in a thin shawl. There was such sadness in her face and in the pinched little face of the baby, that Papa Panov's heart went out to them.

"Won't you come in," he called, stepping outside to meet them. "You both need a warm fire and a rest."

The young mother let him shepherd her indoors and to the comfort of the armchair. She gave a big sigh of relief.

"I'll warm some milk for the baby," Papa Panov said, "I've had children of my own — I can feed her for you." He took the milk from the stove and carefully fed the baby from a spoon, warming her tiny feet by the stove at the same time.

"She needs shoes," the cobbler said.

But the girl replied, "I can't afford shoes. I've got no husband to bring home money. I'm on my way to the next village to get work."

A sudden thought flashed through Papa Panov's mind. He remembered the little shoes he had looked at last night. But he had been keeping those for Jesus. He looked again at the cold little feet and made up his mind.

"Try these on her," he said, handing the baby and the shoes to the mother. The beautiful little shoes were a perfect fit. The girl smiled happily and the baby gurgled with pleasure.

"You have been so kind to us," the girl said, when she got up with her baby to go. "May all your Christmas wishes come true!"

But Papa Panov was beginning to wonder if his very special Christmas wish would come true. Perhaps he had missed his visitor? He looked anxiously up and down the street. There were plenty of people about but they were all faces that he recognized. There were neighbors going to call on their families. They nodded and smiled and wished him Happy Christmas! Or beggars—and Papa Panov hurried indoors to fetch them hot soup and a generous hunk of bread, hurrying out again in case he missed the Important Stranger.

TRIVIA

In many households, part of the fun of eating Christmas pudding is finding a trinket that predicts your fortune for the coming year. For instance, finding a coin means you will become wealthy. Finding a button means you will be a bachelor. A ring means you will get married while a thimble predicts spinsterhood. The idea of hiding something in the pudding comes from the tradition in the Middle Ages of hiding a bean in a cake that was served on Twelfth Night. Whoever found the bean became "king" for the rest of the night.

All too soon the winter dusk fell. When Papa Panov next went to the door and strained his eyes, he could no longer make out the passers-by. Most were home and indoors by now anyway. He walked slowly back into his room at last, put up the shutters, and sat down wearily in his armchair.

So it had been just a dream after all. Jesus had not come.

Then all at once he knew that he was no longer alone in the room.

This was not a dream for he was wide awake. At first he seemed to see before his eyes the long stream of people who had come to him that day. He saw again the old road sweeper, the young mother and her baby and the beggars he had fed. As they passed, each whispered, "Didn't you see me, Papa Panov?"

"Who are you?" he called out, bewildered.

Then another voice answered him. It was the voice from his dream — the voice of Jesus.

"I was hungry and you fed me," he said. "I was naked and you clothed me. I was cold and you warmed me. I came to you today in every one of those you helped and welcomed."

Then all was quiet and still with only the sound of the big clock ticking. A great peace and happiness seemed to fill the room, overflowing Papa Panov's heart until he wanted to burst out singing and laughing and dancing with joy.

"So he did come after all!" was all that he said.

Christmas, my child, is love in action.
DALE EVANS ROGERS

CHRISTMAS CRAFTS AND HOMEMADE GIFTS

Experience the excitement of creating a gift made with your own two hands. Handmade gifts are unique and demonstrate that you care enough to invest time, energy, and creativity into your gift giving.

Snowman from a Lightbulb

MATERIALS LIST:

lightbulb
craft paints — white, red, black, yellow, brown
paintbrushes — one small and one large
craft or floral wire about 12 inches long
baby sock
quick-drying glue
scissors
needle and thread

DIRECTIONS:

1. Paint the glass part white — two coats.
2. Paint in eyes, nose, mouth, and tree limb-type arms, leaving space at the top of the glass for the hat rim and the scarf.
3. Cut the top off the sock, long enough to allow for covering the metal and stitching the top together.

4. Place the sock top inside out, down over the metal, arranging it so that any decoration on the sock will show when it is pulled up.

5. Place one end of the wire around the sock top where the glass meets the metal, and twist tight. Place the other end of the wire around the same place, in the opposite direction so that there is a loop (for hanging the ornament) over the end of the bulb, and twist it tight.

6. Twist the loop tight around the end of the bulb.

7. Pull the sock top up (right side out) over the metal of the bulb.

8. Place a line of glue around the bulb where the glass meets the metal, and gently push the sock onto it to hold the sock in place.

9. Using a needle threaded with matching thread, gather the top of the sock, making sure the loop of the wire protrudes from the middle of the gathered edge, creating a top knot for the hat.

10. From the remaining top of the sock, or from the foot area, cut a band 1 to 1.5 inches wide for the scarf. Cut it open.

11. Glue one end to the front of the snowman, wrap the other end around, and glue that end on top of the first.

12. If necessary, twist the top loop farther around to position the snowman on the tree so that it faces out.

Tip — To personalize the snowman, or have a family of them, cut the face from a snapshot of a child or loved one, and paste it just so it nudges under the cap. Then add stick figure arms instead of the tree limbs, and you have a one-of-a- kind ornament for this year's tree!

Colossal Cookies for Teachers

Decorate extra large sugar cookies. Instead of trying to find giant cookie cutters, you can cut a pattern from paper and trace out the cookies with a knife. Bake first, then add appropriate colors of icing and sprinkles for decorations.

Purchase new Styrofoam meat trays from a local meat market. Red or green plastic wrap works great. Add ribbons or bows for an extra touch.

Wind Chimes

You will need old spoons and forks that you can purchase at a local thrift store or garage sale, scrap wood, fishing line, and children's craft beads. Cut some scrap wood down into squares, about the size of a CD case. Drill a hole in each corner and paint the squares in colors of your choice. Drill holes in the tops of the cutlery and then thread the forks and spoons onto the fishing line. Coordinated colored glass beads can add to the chimes. After adding 10 to 15 beads, thread the remaining line through a hole in the corner of the wood square (so the last bead is right next to the wood), add another two or three beads on the top, and then gather up the four threads and knot them. The chimes make a beautiful tinkling noise when hung in a window or from a tree branch in the backyard.

Christmas Around the World

AUSTRALIA

The first official Christmas Down Under was celebrated on December 25, 1788, at Sydney Cove. Governor Arthur Phillips and his officers dined well, but the majority of the other white inhabitants — the convicts — had bread rations. Christmas in Australia can be very hot. It's not unheard of for the temperature on Christmas Day to approach 100 degrees.

Australians decorate with traditional wreaths, but also with the native Christmas bush and Christmas bells. Other decorations can include Aussie images like kangaroos and koala bears wearing Santa hats or red scarves. Santa is often depicted in swimmers (a swimsuit) and sometimes arrives at Aussie beaches on a surfboard.

The Christmas meal includes a turkey dinner with ham and pork and a flaming Christmas plum pudding for dessert. Another Aussie dessert is pavlova, a combination of strawberries, passion fruit, and whipped cream. Some Australians have their Christmas dinner at midday on a local beach or as a picnic in the backyard.

For many, Christmas begins with midnight mass on Christmas Eve. Seventy percent of Australians are Catholic, Anglican, or Lutheran.

One of the most popular Australian traditions is Carols by Candlelight. Begun in 1937, this group sing-along features tens of thousands of people singing by candlelight. Today, the event is televised from the Arts Centre of the Sidney Myer Music Bowl.

FOOD TRADITIONS

A WORLDWIDE FEAST

Christmas is one of the most celebrated religious holidays around the world. Celebrants often spend months planning the feast and gift giving with family. In some areas the celebration lasts for a week or more. Most observe the season with religious ceremonies and prayer in deference to the Lord Jesus Christ. The day was first recognized as an official feast day in December to commemorate the birth of Jesus by the Bishop of Rome in 137 AD. Julius I, also a Bishop of Rome, selected December 25 as the observance day of Christmas in 350 AD. However, it wasn't that long ago that many countries still had laws against celebrating major religious events. And many countries with predominantly Orthodox faiths celebrate this important birthday thirteen days after December 25, usually on January 7, in accordance with the old Julian calendar. In the United States the early colonies did not celebrate Christmas. As recently as a hundred years ago it was actually illegal to celebrate the holiday in parts of New England. Connecticut even had a law forbidding the baking of mincemeat pies. Obviously the few who did celebrate helped to spread the traditions we now practice.

Christmas was banned in Russia after the 1917 revolution. It wasn't openly observed again until 1992. Today, the faithful participate in all-night mass after the Christmas Eve meal commonly called the "Holy Supper," which begins when the first star appears in the night sky. This meal consists of twelve foods symbolic of the twelve apostles, and some regions add a thirteenth to include Christ. While this is a Lenten meal without meat, it is highly festive in expectation of the Savior's birth, and the continued feasting the next day consists of roast pig or turkey.

Lebanon is the only Middle-Eastern country that celebrates Christmas as an official holiday. Typically, the family will attend midnight mass. Christmas Day is a day of celebration with a holiday dinner including turkey, duck, salads, and pastries.

Christmas feasting includes a wide variety of dishes around the world. Countries obviously have different foods available to theAl, and even within a country there are regional differences. We have tried to give a feel for different meals around the globe, offering menu items from a typical holiday meal; however, due to space constraints you will find only one or two recipes from the meal list. While some will have an ethnic flair, you will find that many are included in the traditional American holiday feast as well.

THE BURGLAR'S CHRISTMAS

WILLA CATHER

Two very shabby looking young men stood at the corner of Prairie Avenue and Eightieth Street, looking despondently at the carriages that whirled by. It was Christmas Eve, and the streets were full of vehicles—florists' wagons, grocers' carts, and carriages. The streets were in that half-liquid, half-congealed condition peculiar to the streets of Chicago at that season of the year. The swift wheels that spun by sometimes threw the slush of mud and snow over the two young men who were talking on the corner.

"Well," remarked the elder of the two, "I guess we are at our rope's end, sure enough. How do you feel?"

"Pretty shaky. The wind's sharp tonight. If I had had anything to eat I mightn't mind it so much. There is simply no show. I'm sick of the whole business. Looks like there's nothing for it but the lake."

"Oh, nonsense, I thought you had more grit. Got anything left you can hock?"

"Nothing but my beard, and I am afraid they wouldn't find it worth a pawn ticket," said the younger man ruefully, rubbing the week's growth of stubble on his face.

"Got any folks anywhere? Now's your time to strike 'em if you have."

"Never mind if I have, they're out of the question."

"Well, you'll be out of it before many hours if you don't make a move of some sort. A man's got to eat. See here, I am going down to Longtin's saloon. I used to play the banjo in there with a couple of fellows, and I'll bone him for some of his free-lunch stuff. You'd better come along, perhaps they'll fill an order for two."

"How far down is it?"

"Well, it's clear downtown, of course, way down on Michigan Avenue."

"Thanks, I guess I'll loaf around here. I don't feel equal to the walk, and the cars—well, the cars are crowded." His features drew themselves into what might have been a smile under happier circumstances.

"No, you never did like street cars, you're too aristocratic. See here, Crawford, I don't like leaving you here. You ain't good company for yourself tonight."

TRIVIA

George Frederick Handel's great Christmas oratorio, Messiah, was first performed in 1742 in the city of Dublin, Ireland. Handel (1685 – 1759) seems to have been a kind and generous man. Messiah was written to aid charities in Ireland. It was a success there from the time of its original performance, though it was not immediately popular in England. Handel's favorite charity in London was the Foundling Hospital. He conducted performances of Messiah there until 1754.

"Crawford? O, yes, that's the last one. There have been so many I forget them."

"Have you got a real name, anyway?"

"O, yes, but it's one of the ones I've forgotten. Don't you worry about me. You go along and get your free lunch. I think I had a row in Longtin's place once. I'd better not show myself there again." As he spoke the young man nodded and turned slowly up the avenue.

He was miserable enough to want to be quite alone. Even the crowd that jostled by him annoyed him. He wanted to think about himself. He had avoided this final reckoning with himself for a year now. He had laughed it off and drunk it off. But now, when all those artificial devices which are employed to turn our thoughts into other channels and shield us from ourselves had failed him, it must come. Hunger is a powerful incentive to introspection.

It is a tragic hour, that hour when we are finally driven to reckon with ourselves, when every avenue of mental distraction has been cut off and our own life and all its ineffaceable failures closes about us like the walls of that old torture chamber of the Inquisition. Tonight, as this man stood stranded in the streets of the city, his hour came. It was not the first time he had been hungry and desperate and alone. But always before there had been some outlook, some chance ahead, some pleasure yet untasted that seemed worth the effort, some face that he fancied was, or would be, dear. But it was not so tonight. The unyielding conviction was upon him that he had failed in everything, had outlived everything. It had been near him for a long time, that Pale Spectre. He had caught its shadow at the bottom of his glass many a time, at the head of his bed when he was sleepless at night, in the twilight shadows when some great sunset broke upon him. It had made life hateful to him when he awoke in the morning before now. But now it settled slowly over him, like night, the endless Northern nights that bid the sun a long farewell. It rose up before him like granite. From this brilliant city with its glad bustle of Yuletide he was shut off as completely as though he were a creature of another species. His days seemed numbered and done, sealed over like the little coral cells at the bottom of the sea. Involuntarily he drew that cold air through his lungs slowly, as though he were tasting it for the last time.

FACTOIDS

When Robert Louis Stevenson, author of Treasure Island, died on December 4, 1894, he willed his November 13 birth date to a friend who disliked her own Christmas birthday.

Yet he was but four and twenty, this man—he looked even younger—and he had a father some place down East who had been very proud of him once. Well, he had taken his life into his own hands, and this was what he had made of it. That was all there was to be said. He could remember the hopeful things they used to say about him at college in the old days, before he had cut away and begun to live by his wits, and he found courage to smile at them now. They had read him wrongly. He knew now that he never had the essentials of success, only the superficial agility that is often mistaken for it. He was tow without the tinder, and he had burnt himself out at other people's fires. He had helped other people to make it win, but he himself—he had never touched an enterprise that had not failed eventually. Or, if it survived his connection with it, it left him behind.

The joy of brightening other lives, bearing each other's burdens, easing other's loads and supplanting empty hearts and lives with generous gifts becomes for us the magic of Christmas.

W.C. JONES

His last venture had been with some ten-cent specialty company, a little lower than all the others, that had gone to pieces in Buffalo, and he had worked his way to Chicago by boat. When the boat made up its crew for the outward voyage, he was dispensed with as usual. He was used to that. The reason for it? O, there are so many reasons for failure! His was a very common one.

As he stood there in the wet under the street light he drew up his reckoning with the world and decided that it had treated him as well as he deserved. He had overdrawn his account once too often. There had been a day when he thought otherwise; when he had said he was unjustly handled, that his failure was merely the lack of proper adjustment between himself and other men, that some day he would be recognized and it would all come right. But he knew better than that now, and he was still man enough to bear no grudge against any one— man or woman.

Tonight was his birthday, too. There seemed something particularly amusing in that. He turned up a limp little coat collar to try to keep a little of the wet chill from his throat, and instinctively began to remember all the birthday parties he used to have. He was so cold and empty that his mind seemed unable to grapple with any serious question. He kept thinking about gingerbread and frosted cakes like a child. He could remember the splendid birthday parties his mother used to give him, when all the other little boys in the block came in their Sunday clothes and creaking shoes, with their ears still red from their mother's towel, and the pink and white birthday cake, and the stuffed olives and all the dishes of which he had been particularly fond, and how he would eat and eat and then go to bed and dream of Santa Claus. And in the morning he would awaken and eat again, until by night the family doctor arrived with his castor oil, and poor William used to dolefully say that it was altogether too much to have your birthday and Christmas all at once. He could remember, too, the royal birthday suppers he had given at college, and the stag dinners, and the toasts, and the music, and the good fellows who had wished him happiness and really meant what they said.

FOR FUN

My next-door neighbor and her mother-in-law went to a huge outlet mall just days before Christmas. Her mother-in-law tripped and scraped her elbow and face on the pavement. My neighbor helped her mother-in-law back into the car and tried to shut the car door so that she could take her to a minor emergency clinic. Her mother-in-law stuck her leg out and said, "We can't leave now! We have such a great parking space!"

And since then there were other birthday suppers that he could not remember so clearly; the memory of them was heavy and flat, like cigarette smoke that has been shut in a room all night, like champagne that has been a day opened, a song that has been too often sung, an acute sensation that has been overstrained. They seemed tawdry and garish, discordant to him now. He rather wished he could forget them altogether.

Whichever way his mind now turned there was one thought that it could not escape, and that was the idea of food. He caught the scent of a cigar suddenly, and felt a sharp pain in the pit of his abdomen and a sudden moisture in his mouth. His cold hands clenched angrily, and for a moment he felt that bitter hatred of wealth, of ease, of everything that is well fed and well housed that is common to starving men. At any rate he had a right to eat! He had demanded great things from the world once: fame and wealth and admiration. Now it was simply bread—and he would have it! He looked about him quickly and felt the blood begin to stir in his veins. In all his straits he had never stolen anything; his tastes were above it. But tonight there would be no tomorrow. He was amused at the way in which the idea excited him. Was it possible there was yet one more experience that would distract him, one thing that had power to excite his jaded interest? Good! He had failed at everything else, now he would see what his chances would be as a common thief. It would be amusing to watch the beautiful consistency of his destiny work itself out even in that role. It would be interesting to add another study to his gallery of futile attempts, and then label them all: "the failure as a journalist," "the failure as a lecturer," "the failure as a business man," "the failure as a thief," and so on.

A girl hastened by him with her arms full of packages. She walked quickly and nervously, keeping well within the shadow, as if she were not accustomed to carrying bundles and did not care to meet any of her friends. As she crossed the muddy street, she made an effort to lift her skirt a little, and as she did so one of the packages slipped unnoticed from beneath her arm. He caught it up and overtook her. "Excuse me, but I think you dropped something."

What is Christinas? It is tenderness for the past, courage tor the present, hope for the future. It is a fervent wish that every tup may overflow with blessings rich and eternal, and that every path may lead to peace.

AGNES M. PHARO

She started, "Oh, yes, thank you, I would rather have lost anything than that."

The young man turned angrily upon himself. The package must have contained something of value. Why had he not kept it? Was this the sort of thief he would make? He ground his teeth together. There is nothing more maddening than to have morally consented to crime and then lack the nerve force to carry it out.

A carriage drove up to the house before which he stood. Several richly dressed women alighted and went in. It was a new house, and must have been built since he was in Chicago last. The front door was open and he could see down the hallway and up the staircase. The servant had left the door and gone with the guests. The first floor was brilliantly lighted, but the windows upstairs were dark. It looked very easy, just to slip upstairs to the darkened chambers where the jewels and trinkets of the fashionable occupants were kept.

Still burning with impatience against himself he entered quickly. Instinctively he removed his mud-stained hat as he passed quickly and quietly up the staircase. It struck him as being a rather superfluous courtesy in a burglar, but he had done it before he had thought. His way was clear enough, he met no one on the stairway or in the upper hall. The gas was lit in the upper hall. He passed the first chamber door through sheer cowardice. The second he entered quickly, thinking of something else lest his courage should fail him, and closed the door behind him. The light from the hall shone into the room through the transom. The apartment was furnished richly enough to justify his expectations. He went at once to the dressing case. A number of rings and small trinkets lay in a silver tray. These he put hastily in his pocket. He opened the upper drawer and found, as he expected, several leather cases. In the first he opened was a lady's watch, in the second a pair of old-fashioned bracelets; he seemed to dimly remember having seen bracelets like them before, somewhere. The third case was heavier, the spring was much worn, and it opened easily. It held a cup of some kind. He held it up to the light and then his strained nerves gave way and he uttered a sharp exclamation. It was the silver mug he used to drink from when he was a little boy.

TRIVIA

As early as 1822, the postmaster in Washington DC was worried by the amount of extra mail at Christmas time. His preferred solution to the problem was to limit by law the number of cards a person could send. Even though commercial cards were not available at that time, people were already sending so many homemade cards that sixteen extra postmen had to he hired in the city.

The door opened, and a woman stood in the doorway facing him. She was a tall woman, with white hair, in evening dress. The light from the hall streamed in upon him, but she was not afraid. She stood looking at him a moment, then she threw out her hand and went quickly toward him.

"Willie, Willie! Is it you?"

He struggled to loose her arms from him, to keep her lips from his cheek. "Mother—you must not! You do not understand! O, my God, this is worst of all!" Hunger, weakness, cold, shame, all came back to him, and shook his self-control completely. Physically he was too weak to stand a shock like this. Why could it not have been an ordinary discovery, arrest, the station house and all the rest of it. Anything but this! A hard dry sob broke from him. Again he strove to disengage himself.

"Who is it says I shall not kiss my son? O, my boy, we have waited so long for this! You have been so long in coming, even I almost gave you up."

Her lips upon his cheek burnt him like fire. He put his hand to his throat, and spoke thickly and incoherently:

"You do not understand. I did not know you were here. I came here to rob — it is the first time — I swear it — but I am a common thief. My pockets are full of your jewels now. Can't you hear me? I am a common thief!"

"Hush, my boy, those are ugly words. How could you rob your own house? How could you take what is your own? They are all yours, my son, as wholly yours as my great love — and you can't doubt that, Will, do you?"

That soft voice, the warmth and fragrance of her person stole through his chill, empty veins like a gentle stimulant. He felt as though all his strength were leaving him and even consciousness. He held fast to her and bowed his head on her strong shoulder, and groaned aloud. "O, mother, life is hard, hard!"

This is Christmas: not the tinsel, not the giving and receiving, not even the carols, but the humble heart that receives anew the wondrous gift, the Christ.
FRANK MCKIBBEN

She said nothing, but held him closer. And oh, the strength of those white arms that held him! O, the assurance of safety in that warm bosom that rose and fell under his cheek! For a moment they stood so, silently. Then they heard a heavy step upon the stair. She led him to a chair and went out and closed the door. At the top of the staircase she met a tall, broad-shouldered man, with iron gray hair, and a face alert and stern. Her eyes were shining and her cheeks on fire, her whole face was one expression of intense determination.

"James, it is William in there, come home. You must keep him at any cost. If he goes this time, I go with him. Oh, James, be easy with him, he has suffered so." She broke from a command to an entreaty, and laid her hand on his shoulder. He looked questioningly at her a moment, then went in the room and quietly shut the door.

She stood leaning against the wall, clasping her temples with her hands and listening to the low indistinct sound of the voices within. Her own lips moved silently. She waited a long time, scarcely breathing. At last the door opened, and her husband came out. He stopped to say in a shaken voice, "You go to him now, he will stay. I will go to my room. I will see him again in the morning."

She put her arm about his neck, "Oh, James, I thank you, I thank you! This is the night he came so long ago, you remember? I gave him to you then, and now you give him back to me!"

Christmas is not a time nor a season, but a state of mind. To cherish peace and goodwill, to be plenteous in mercy, is to have the real spirit of Christmas.
CALVIN COOLIDGE

"Don't, Helen," he muttered. "He is my son, I have never forgotten that. I failed with him. I don't like to fail, it cuts my pride. Take him and make a man of him." He passed on down the hall.

She flew into the room where the young man sat with his head bowed upon his knee. She dropped upon her knees beside him. Ah, it was so good to him to feel those arms again!

"He is so glad, Willie, so glad! He may not show it, but he is as happy as I. He never was demonstrative with either of us, you know."

"Oh, my God, he was good enough," groaned the man. "I told him everything, and he was good enough. I don't see how either of you can look at me, speak to me, touch me." He shivered under her clasp again as when she had first touched him, and tried weakly to throw her off.

But she whispered softly, "This is my right, my son."

Presently, when he was calmer, she rose. "Now, come with me into the library, and I will have your dinner brought there."

As they went downstairs she remarked apologetically, "I will not call Ellen tonight; she has a number of guests to attend to. She is a big girl now, you know, and came out last winter. Besides, I want you all to myself tonight."

When the dinner came, and it came very soon, he fell upon it savagely. As he ate she told him all that had transpired during the years of his absence, and how his father's business had brought them there. "I was glad when we came. I thought you would drift West. I seemed a good deal nearer to you here."

There was a gentle unobtrusive sadness in her tone that was too soft for a reproach. "Have you everything you want? It is a comfort to see you eat."

He smiled grimly, "It is certainly a comfort to me. I have not indulged in this frivolous habit for some thirty-five hours."

She caught his hand and pressed it sharply, uttering a quick remonstrance. "Don't say that! I know, but I can't hear you say it—it's too terrible! My boy, food has choked me many a time when I have thought of the possibility of that. Now take the old lounging chair by the fire, and if you are too tired to talk, we will just sit and rest together."

He sank into the depths of the big leather chair with the lions' heads on the arms, where he had sat so often in the days when his feet did not touch the floor and he was half afraid of the grim monsters cut in the polished wood. That chair seemed to speak to him of things long forgotten. It was like the touch of an old familiar friend. He felt a sudden yearning tenderness for the happy little boy who had sat there and dreamed of the big world so long ago. Alas, he had been dead many a summer, that little boy!

FACTOIDS

Yuletide-named towns in the United States include Santa Claus, located both in Arizona and Indiana; Noel in Missouri; and Christmas in both Arizona and Florida.

He sat looking up at the magnificent woman beside him. He had almost forgotten how handsome she was; how lustrous and sad were the eyes that were set under that serene brow, how impetuous and wayward the mouth even now, how superb the white throat and shoulders! Ah, the wit and grace and fineness of this woman! He remembered how proud he had been of her as a boy when she came to see him at school. Then in the deep red coals of the grate he saw the faces of other women who had come since then into his vexed, disordered life. Laughing faces, with eyes artificially bright, eyes without depth or meaning, features without the stamp of high sensibilities. And he had left this face for such as those!

He sighed restlessly and laid his hand on hers. There seemed refuge and protection in the touch of her, as in the old days when he was afraid of the dark. He had been in the dark so long now, his confidence was so thoroughly shaken, and he was bitterly afraid of the night and of himself.

"Ah, mother, you make other things seem so false. You must feel that I owe you an explanation, but I can't make any, even to myself. Ah, but we make poor exchanges in life. I can't make out the riddle of it all. Yet there are things I ought to tell you before I accept your confidence like this."

"I'd rather you wouldn't, Will. Listen: Between you and me there can be no secrets. We are more alike than other people. Dear boy, I know all about it. I am a woman, and circumstances were different with me, but we are of one blood. I have lived all your life before you. You have never had an impulse that I have not known, you have never touched a brink that my feet have not trod. This is your birthday night.

FOR FUN

A teacher asked her Sunday School class to draw pictures of their favorite Bible stories. She was puzzled by one child's picture, which showed four people on an airplane, so she asked him which story it was meant to represent.
"The flight to Egypt," he responded.
"I see. And that must be Mary, Joseph, and Baby Jesus," the teacher replied. "But who's the fourth person?"
"Oh, that's Pontius — the Pilot."

Twenty-four years ago I foresaw all this. I was a young woman then and I had hot battles of my own, and I felt your likeness to me. You were not like other babies. From the hour you were born you were restless and discontented, as I had been before you. You used to brace your strong little limbs against mine and try to throw me off as you did tonight. Tonight you have come back to me, just as you always did after you ran away to swim in the river that was forbidden you, the river you loved because it was forbidden. You are tired and sleepy, just as you used to be then, only a little older and a little paler and a little more foolish. I never asked you where you had been then, nor will I now. You have come back to me, that's all in all to me. I know your every possibility and limitation, as a composer knows his instrument."

He found no answer that was worthy to give to talk like this. He had not found life easy since he had lived by his wits. He had come to know poverty at close quarters. He had known what it was to be gay with an empty pocket, to wear violets in his buttonhole when he had not breakfasted, and all the hateful shams of the poverty of idleness. He had been a reporter on a big metropolitan daily, where men grind out their brains on paper until they have not one idea left—and still grind on. He had worked in a real estate office, where ignorant men were swindled.

He had sung in a comic opera chorus and played Harris in an Uncle Tom's Cabin company, and edited a socialist weekly. He had been dogged by debt and hunger and grinding poverty, until to sit here by a warm fire without concern as to how it would be paid for seemed unnatural.

He looked up at her questioningly. "I wonder if you know how much you pardon?"

"Oh, my poor boy, much or little, what does it matter? Have you wandered so far and paid such a bitter price for knowledge and not yet learned that love has nothing to do with pardon or forgiveness, that it only loves, and loves—and loves?

Christmas is the season for kindling the fire of hospitality in the hall, the genial frame of charity in the heart.
WASHINGTON IRVING

They have not taught you well, the women of your world." She leaned over and kissed him, as no woman had kissed him since he left her.

He drew a long sigh of rich content. The old life, with all its bitterness and useless antagonism and flimsy sophistries, its brief delights that were always tinged with fear and distrust and unfaith, that whole miserable, futile, swindled world of Bohemia seemed immeasurably distant and far away, like a dream that is over and done. And as the chimes rang joyfully outside and sleep pressed heavily upon his eyelids, he wondered dimly if the Author of this sad little riddle of ours were not able to solve it after all, and if the Potter would not finally mete out his all comprehensive justice, such as none but he could have, to his Things of Clay, which are made in his own patterns, weak or strong, for his own ends; and if some day we will not awaken and find that all evil is a dream, a mental distortion that will pass when the dawn shall break.

TRIVIA

At lavish Christmas feasts in the Middle Ages, swans and peacocks were sometimes served "endored." This meant the flesh was painted with saffron dissolved in melted butter. In addition to their painted flesh, endored birds were served wrapped in their own skin and feathers, which had keen removed and set aside prior to roasting.

Traditions

THE TRADITION OF THE CHRISTMAS STOCKING

Whether personalized, elegant, traditional red trimmed in white, store-bought or homemade, nothing says Christinas more than a Christmas stocking.

There are many legends behind the Christmas stocking. One story involves a kind nobleman who lost everything after his wife died of a long illness. He had invested unwisely in various inventions, and ultimately he and his three daughters had to move into a small cottage and live quite poorly. Without dowries, the daughters would never be able to marry, and they lived with no hope.

One evening after the daughters had washed their poor dresses and stockings, they hung the stockings on the fireplace to dry overnight. Saint Nicholas came by their house after they had gone to bed and, seeing the stockings hanging by the fire, was inspired to give them some anonymous help. He managed, somehow, to drop three small bags filled with gold down the chimney and into the stockings, where the daughters found them on Christmas morning. The daughters were able to use the money for dowries. According to the story, each daughter married well, and they and their father lived long, and happy lives.

There are other stories from different countries involving boxes, shoes, clogs, and other containers filled with food, treats, or gifts during the Christmas season. In fact, there are as many variations of the stocking as there are cultures, with a great many of them involving leaving a treat for someone or something (Santa's reindeer, the three wise men's camels), and waking to a shoe, box, or stocking filled with some sort of gilt as a reward for that kindness. Today, children hang empty stockings and watch them fill up with various small gifts and surprises to be opened along with other gifts on Christmas Eve or Christmas Day. They bring joy to the recipients, and during the Christmas season provide a decorative touch wherever they are hung.

FOOD TRADITIONS

UNITED STATES

Here a traditional meal will usually include a main entree of turkey, goose, or ham; even a standing rib roast is not uncommon. Side dishes of stuffing or dressing, mashed potatoes, green bean casserole, sweet potatoes or candied yams, fruit and pies for dessert round out the table and our belts.

Candied Yams

INGREDIENTS:

3 large sweet potatoes (about 3.5 pounds)
1 20-ounce can of pineapple chunks in their own juice
1 small orange, sliced
1/2 medium-size lemon, sliced
1 cup packed dark-brown sugar
1/2 cup dark seedless raisins
4 tablespoons margarine or butter (1/2 stick)
1/2 teaspoon ground cinnamon
1/2 teaspoon ground nutmeg
1/2 teaspoon ground allspice
1 15-ounce can of mandarin orange sections
2 medium-size firm bananas, sliced
1/2 cup pecans, toasted and chopped
1/2 cup miniature marshmallows

DIRECTIONS:

In a 5-quart pot over high heat, cook sweet potatoes and enough water to cover until boiling. Reduce heat to low, cover and simmer 30 to 40 minutes, until potatoes are fork-tender. Drain potatoes; cool slightly until easy to handle, then peel and cut potatoes into 1/2-inch-thick slices.

Meanwhile, drain pineapple chunks and discard all but 1/2 cup juice. In 3-quart saucepan over high heat, cook pineapple juice, orange and lemon slices, brown sugar, raisins, margarine or butter, cinnamon, nutmeg, and allspice to boiling. Reduce heat to low, cover and simmer until mixture thickens slightly, about 10 minutes. Discard orange and lemon slices.

Preheat oven to 350 degrees F. Grease 13 x 9-inch glass baking dish. Arrange sweet potato slices, overlapping in baking dish. Tuck pineapple chunks, mandarin oranges, bananas, and pecans among sweet potato slices. Pour spice sauce over potatoes; top with marshmallows. Bake 20 to 25 minutes until marshmallows melt and turn golden brown and the mixture is hot and bubbly.

FOOD TRADITIONS

GREAT BRITAIN

A medieval English Christmas dinner would include brawn headcheese, roast peacock or swan, boar's head, and mutton pie (precursor to the modern mince pie). Today, dinner usually consists of turkey, goose, or chicken with stuffing; roast potatoes; mince pies; fruitcakes; and plum pudding.

Mrs. Beeton's Rich Plum Pudding

The name "plum pudding" continues to be used even though many recipes call for raisins, currants, nuts, and sultanas instead of prunes. It is often served with custard or brandy butter, with brandy poured over the pudding and set aflame while carried to the table. This recipe was taken from a 1923 cookbook.

INGREDIENTS:

8 ounces chopped suet (raw beef or mutton fat, especially the fat found around the loins and kidneys) or modern-day equivalent

8 ounces bread crumbs

2 ounces plain flour

8 ounces raisins

8 ounces sultanas

4 ounces currants

4 ounces candied peel (cut your own or use ready cut)

half a grated nutmeg

half an ounce of mixed spice

half an ounce of ground cinnamon

1 gill (about a quarter pint) milk

1 wineglass rum or brandy (optional)

2 ounces desiccated coconut or shredded almonds

1 lemon

4 eggs

pinch of salt

DIRECTIONS:

Grease 1 basin.

Skin the suet or chop it finely. Clean the fruit, stone the raisins, shred the mixed peel; peel and chop the lemon rind.

Put all the dry ingredients in a basin and mix well. Add the milk, stir in the eggs one at a time, add the rum or brandy and the strained juice of a lemon.

Work the whole thoroughly for some minutes, so that the ingredients are all well blended.

Put the mixture in a well-greased or floured pudding cloth. Boil for 4 hours or steam for at least 5 hours.

(This recipe has no baking powder or sugar mentioned. Makes 8 to 9 servings. Note: 1 gill is a quarter pint or 5 fluid ounces or 150 milliliters.)

Yorkshire Pudding

This recipe is adapted from the *New York Times Cookbook* edited by Craig Claiborne.

INGREDIENTS:

2 eggs
1 cup whole milk
1 cup flour
1/2 teaspoon salt
1/4 cup beef drippings

DIRECTIONS:

Preheat oven to 450 degrees F. Pour beef drippings into an 11 x 7-inch baking or roasting pan and brush drippings over bottom and sides of pan. Place pan in the oven to heat. Beat the eggs with the milk. Sift together flour and salt. Stir into egg mixture. Beat batter until well blended. When the drippings are sizzling hot, remove the pan and pour batter into it. Place back in oven and bake for 20 to 25 minutes. Remove from oven and cut into squares. Best when served immediately.

Irish Roast Goose

This recipe is adapted from Darina Allen's *Festive Foods of Ireland* cookbook. Ms. Allen runs the world-renowned Ballymaloe Cookery School in County Cork.

INGREDIENTS:

1 goose weighing about 10 pounds with giblets, neck, heart, and gizzard (Note: While a goose looks quite big, it has a large cavity, so allow 1 pound of uncooked weight per person.)
1 small onion 1 carrot
bouquet garni containing:
1 sprig of thyme
3 or 4 parsley stalks
1 small piece of celery
6 or 7 peppercorns
roux, if desired, for thickening

STUFFING:

2 pounds potatoes
1/2 stick butter
1 pound onions
1 pound Granny Smith cooking apples, peeled and chopped
1 tablespoon chopped parsley
1.5 tablespoons lemon balm
salt and freshly ground pepper

DIRECTIONS:

Scrub potatoes and boil in salt water until cooked. Drain water and mash potatoes, including skins. Melt butter and simmer onions in covered saucepan over gentle heat for 5 minutes.

Add apples and cook until they break down into a fluff, then stir in the mashed potatoes and herbs.

Season with salt and pepper. Allow to get quite cold before stuffing goose.

GOOSE:

Remove giblets, neck, heart, and gizzard from goose cavity. Put goose into large saucepan with giblets, onion, carrot, bouquet garni, and peppercorns. Cover with cold water, bring to a boil, and simmer for about 2 hours. Remove bird from stock, pat dry, and place in roasting pan. Strain stock and store in refrigerator until time to make gravy. Preheat oven to 350 degrees F. Season goose cavity with salt and pepper and fill with cold stuffing. Sprinkle sea salt over breast and rub into skin. Roast for 2 to 2.5 hours. During roasting, pour off excess fat three or four times.

(Store fat in refrigerator—it keeps for months and is wonderful for roasting or sautéing potatoes). To test whether goose is cooked, prick the thigh at the thickest part. If the juices that run out are clear, it's ready. If they're pink, it needs a little longer. When the bird is cooked, remove to a large oven-proof platter and place in oven on low heat to keep warm while you make the gravy.

GRAVY:

Pour or spoon off remaining fat in pan. Add about 2 cups of strained giblet stock to roasting pan. Bring to a boil, and, using a small whisk, scrape the pan well to dissolve any meaty deposits. Taste for seasoning and, if desired, thicken with a little roux. If the gravy seems weak, boil for a few minutes to concentrate the flavor. If it seems too strong, add a little more water or stock

Makes 8 to 10 servings.

CHRISTMAS CRAFTS AND HOMEMADE GIFTS

A Slice of Christmas

Cut a slice off the bottom of your tree trunk. Sand it down on both sides and drill a hole at the top. Take a family picture in front of the Christmas tree and decoupage this picture on one side. Put the date on the other side and decoupage it as well.

Craft Box

Purchase a cardboard hatbox or take a large shoe box and fill it with odds and ends that can be used to make things. Consider who the gift is for and choose colors and items that you know they will enjoy: pencils, pens, crayons, beads, thread, cotton balls, tissue paper, glue, markers, paper, ribbons, buttons, and more. Be creative.

Magnets for the Refrigerator

Choose several favorite photos, and print them in the size that will fit in a clear plastic frame with a magnet on the back (available at discount stores or drug stores). It's easy to pull photos from special times and proud moments with the person you're creating the gift.

Chocolate Spoons

Purchase a bag of plastic spoons. Melt cooking chocolate and dip the spoons in one at a time, covering the "spoon" portion with chocolate and holding it over the saucepan or bowl until it stops dripping. Lay them on foil to harden properly. Once they're cool, wrap them in clear cellophane and tie the top with some curling ribbon, with a tag attached and instructions to stir through hot coffee until the chocolate has melted. These can be grouped nicely in a small basket with specialty coffees, or in a new coffee mug.

Christmas Around the World

BETHLEHEM

In Bethlehem, the Church of the Nativity is decorated with flags. On Christmas Eve, people watch the dramatic annual procession. Galloping horsemen and police mounted on Arabian horses lead the parade followed by a solitary horseman carrying a cross and sitting astride a coal black steed. Next, the churchmen and government officials arrive. The procession solemnly enters and places an ancient effigy of the Christ Child in the church. Deep, winding stairs lead to a grotto where visitors find a silver star marking the site of the birth of Jesus.

Christian homes in Bethlehem are marked by a cross painted over the door and a homemade manger scene on display. A star is set up on a pole in the village square.

THE ELVES AND THE SHOEMAKER

THE BROTHERS GRIMM

Once upon a time in a village far away, there was a poor shoemaker and his wife. The shoemaker worked very hard but there was never enough money. At last, one night, they had no food for their supper. "All I have is enough leather to make one pair of shoes," he told his wife. He cut out the leather and placed it on the table. "I will make them in the morning," he said. And they went to bed hungry. In the morning, to his surprise, the leather had been made into a beautiful pair of shoes.

Just then, a customer came in. "I have never seen such beautiful shoes!" she said. She gave the shoemaker three gold coins for them. With the money, the shoemaker's wife bought food and made a delicious dinner. The shoemaker bought more leather. That night, he cut the leather for two pairs of shoes.

In the morning, there were two pairs of shoes on the table! Soon two customers came in and bought the shoes. They each paid him well. So the shoemaker bought leather enough for three pairs more.

He cut out the work again that night, and found it finished in the morning. And so it went on for some time. Whatever he got ready at night was always done by morning, and the good man soon was rich.

One evening, at Christmas-time, he said to his wife, "Tonight let's sit up and watch, to see who it is that comes and does my work for me." So they hid themselves behind a curtain to see what would happen.

As soon as the clock struck midnight, in came two little elves. They sat on the shoemaker's bench and went to work. They stitched and rapped and hammered and tapped at such a rate that the shoemaker was amazed, and could not take his eyes off them for a moment.

On they went until the job was done, and the shoes stood ready on the table. Then they ran away as quick as lightning.

The next day the shoemaker said, "The elves have helped us. How can we help them?"

"I have an idea," said his wife.

"It is so cold outside, and they have no coats to wear. I will make each of them a coat and a hat. And you can make each of them a little pair of shoes."

And so they did. That night they put two little hats and two little coats and two little pairs of shoes on the table. Then they went and hid behind the curtain to watch what the elves would do.

As the clock struck midnight, the elves came in and were going to sit down at their work as usual. But when they saw the clothes lying there for them, they laughed! They dressed themselves in the twinkling of an eye, and danced and skipped and sprang about as merry as could be.

At last they danced out the door. The shoemaker and his wife never saw them again. But everything went well with them as long as they lived.

FACTOIDS

The popular Christmas song "Jingle Bells" was composed in 1857 by James Pierpont and was originally called "One Horse Open Sleigh."

CHRISTMAS CRAFTS AND HOMEMADE GIFTS

THEMED GIFT BASKETS

Choose items with a theme for gift baskets. Put items in an inexpensive basket or wrap them with ribbon. (Don't forget the dollar stores when shopping.) Here are a few themes to build your gift giving around:

1. *Specialty pastas, a jar of your favorite spaghetti sauce, breadsticks, and fresh brownies for an easy meal*
2. *Gourmet coffees with a personal coffee mug*
3. *Disposable camera or rolls of film*
4. *Teacup with a box of herbal teas*
5. *Home-baked bread with the recipe*
6. *Nuts — almonds, pecans, pistachios, and peanuts*
7. *Small photo fames and mini albums with special photos*
8. *Stationery and gel pens*
9. *Basket of deli cheese and fruit*
10. *Gardening gloves with a plant or flower seeds*
11. *Homemade cookie mix with instructions for baking*
12. *Gourmet popcorn and flavored oil*
13. *Locally made barbecue or steak sauce with a basting brush*
14. *Set of dish towels and dish cloths*
15. *Movie theater gift certificates*
16. *Collectible sports cards*
17. *Address book and prepaid long-distance phone cards*
18. *Expensive socks, still under $10*
19. *Special soaps and bath puff*
20. *Video/DVD rental gift certificates*

THE GIFT OF THE MAGI

O. HENRY

One dollar and eighty-seven cents. That was all. And sixty cents of it was in pennies. Pennies saved one and two at a time by bulldozing the grocer and the vegetable man and the butcher until one's cheeks burned with the silent imputation of parsimony that such close dealing implied. Three times Della counted it. One dollar and eighty-seven cents. And the next day would be Christmas.

There was clearly nothing to do but flop down on the shabby little couch and howl. So Della did it. Which instigates the moral reflection that life is made up of sobs, sniffles, and smiles, with sniffles predominating.

While the mistress of the home is gradually subsiding from the first stage to the second, take a look at the home. A furnished flat at $8 per week. It did not exactly beggar description, but it certainly had that word on the lookout for the mendicancy squad.

In the vestibule below was a letter-box into which no letter would go, and an electric button from which no mortal finger could coax a ring. Also appertaining thereunto was a card bearing the name "Mr. James Dillingham Young."

The "Dillingham" had been flung to the breeze during a former period of prosperity when its possessor was being paid $30 per week. Now, when the income was shrunk to $20, though, they were thinking seriously of contracting to a modest and unassuming D.

But whenever Mr. James Dillingham Young came home and reached his flat above he was called "Jim" and greatly hugged by Mrs. James Dillingham Young, already introduced to you as Della. Which is all very good.

Della finished her cry and attended to her cheeks with the powder rag. She stood by the window and looked out dully at a gray cat walking a gray fence in a gray backyard. Tomorrow would be Christmas Day, and she had only $1.87 with which to buy Jim a present. She had been saving every penny she could for months, with this result. Twenty dollars a week doesn't go far. Expenses had been greater than she had calculated. They always are. Only $1.87 to buy a present for Jim. Her Jim. Many a happy hour she had spent planning for something nice for him. Something fine and rare and sterling — something just a little bit near to being worthy of the honor of being owned by Jim.

There was a pier-glass between the windows of the room. Perhaps you have seen a pier-glass in an $8 flat. A very thin and very agile person may, by observing his reflection in a rapid sequence of longitudinal strips, obtain a fairly accurate conception of his looks. Della, being slender, had mastered the art.

Suddenly she whirled from the window and stood before the glass. Her eyes were shining brilliantly, but her face had lost its color within twenty seconds. Rapidly she pulled down her hair and let it fall to its full length.

The best of all gifts around any Christmas tree: the presence of a
happy family all wrapped up in each other.
BURTON HILLIS

Now, there were two possessions of the James Dillingham Youngs in which they both took a mighty pride. One was Jim's gold watch that had been his father's and his grandfather's. The other was Della's hair. Had the queen of Sheba lived in the flat across the airshaft, Della would have let her hair hang out the window some day to dry just to depreciate Her Majesty's jewels and gifts. Had King Solomon been the janitor, with all his treasures piled up in the basement, Jim would have pulled out his watch every time he passed, just to see him pluck at his beard from envy.

So now Della's beautiful hair fell about her rippling and shining like a cascade of brown waters. It reached below her knee and made itself almost a garment for her. And then she did it up again nervously and quickly. Once she faltered for a minute and stood still while a tear or two splashed on the worn red carpet.

TRIVIA

Postmen in Victorian England were popularly called "robins." This was because their uniforms were red. The British Post Office grew out of the practice of carrying royal dispatches. Red was considered a royal color, so uniforms and letter-boxes were red. Christmas cards often showed a robin delivering Christmas mail.

On went her old brown jacket; on went her old brown hat. With a whirl of skirts and with the brilliant sparkle still in her eyes, she fluttered out the door and down the stairs to the street.

Where she stopped the sign read: "Mne. Sofronie. Hair Goods of All Kinds." One flight up Della ran, and collected herself, panting. Madame, large, too white, chilly, hardly looked the "Sofronie."

"Will you buy my hair?" asked Della.

"I buy hair," said Madame. "Take yer hat off and let's have a sight at the looks of it."

Down rippled the brown cascade.

"Twenty dollars," said Madame, lifting the mass with a practiced hand.

"Give it to me quick," said Della.

Oh, and the next two hours tripped by on rosy wings. Forget the hashed metaphor. She was ransacking the stores for Jim's present.

She found it at last. It surely had been made for Jim and no one else. There was no other like it in any of the stores, and she had turned all of them inside out. It was a platinum fob chain simple and chaste in design, properly proclaiming its value by substance alone and not by meretricious ornamentation — as all good things should do. It was even worthy of The Watch. As soon as she saw it she knew that it must be Jim's. It was like him. Quietness and value — the description applied to both. Twenty-one dollars they took from her for it, and she hurried home with the 87 cents. With that chain on his watch Jim might be properly anxious about the time in any company. Grand as the watch was, he sometimes looked at it on the sly on account of the old leather strap that he used in place of a chain.

When Della reached home her intoxication gave way a little to prudence and reason.

She got out her curling irons and lighted the gas and went to work repairing the ravages made by generosity added to love. Which is always a tremendous task, dear friends — a mammoth task.

Within forty minutes her head was covered with tiny, close-lying curls that made her look wonderfully like a truant schoolboy. She looked at her reflection in the mirror long, carefully, and critically.

"If Jim doesn't kill me," she said to herself, "before he takes a second look at me, he'll say I look like a Coney Island chorus girl. But what could I do — oh! what could I do with a dollar and eighty-seven cents?"

At 7 o'clock the coffee was made and the frying-pan was on the back of the stove hot and ready to cook the chops.

FOR FUN

Christmas: When you exchange hellos with strangers and good buys with friends.

Jim was never late. Della doubled the fob chain in her hand and sat on the corner of the table near the door that he always entered. Then she heard his step on the stair away down on the first flight, and she turned white for just a moment. She had a habit for saying little silent prayers about the simplest everyday things, and now she whispered: "Please God, make him think I am still pretty."

The door opened and Jim stepped in and dosed it. He looked thin and very serious. Poor fellow, he was only twenty-two—and to be burdened with a family! He needed a new overcoat and he was without gloves.

Jim stopped inside the door, as immovable as a setter at the scent of quail. His eyes were fixed upon Della, and there was an expression in them that she could not read, and it terrified her. It was not anger, nor surprise, nor disapproval, nor horror, nor any of the sentiments that she had been prepared for. He simply stared at her fixedly with that peculiar expression on his face.

Della wriggled off the table and went for him.

"Jim, darling," she cried, "don't look at me that way. I had my hair cut off and sold because I couldn't have lived through Christmas without giving you a present. It'll grow out again—you won't mind, will you? I just had to do it. My hair grows awfully fast. Say 'Merry Christmas!' Jim, and let's be happy. You don't know what a nice—what a beautiful, nice gift I've got for you."

"You've cut off your hair?" asked Jim, laboriously, as if he had not arrived at that patent fact yet even after the hardest mental labor.

FACTOIDS

In 1752, eleven days were dropped from the year when the switch from the Julian calendar to the Gregorian calendar was made. The December 25 date was effectively moved eleven days backward. Some Christian church sects, called old calendarises, still celebrate Christmas on January 7

"Cut it off and sold it," said Della. "Don't you like me just as well, anyhow? I'm me without my hair, ain't I?"

Jim looked about the room curiously.

"You say your hair is gone?" he said, with an air almost of idiocy.

"You needn't look for it," said Della. "It's sold, I tell you—sold and gone, too. It's Christmas Eve, boy. Be good to me, for it went for you. Maybe the hairs of my head were numbered," she went on with sudden serious sweetness, "but nobody could ever count my love for you. Shall I put the chops on, Jim?"

Out of his trance Jim seemed quickly to wake. He enfolded his Della. For ten seconds let us regard with discreet scrutiny some inconsequential object in the other direction. Eight dollars a week or a million a year—what is the difference? A mathematician or a wit would give you the wrong answer. The magi brought valuable gifts, but that was not among them. This dark assertion will be illuminated later on.

Jim drew a package from his overcoat pocket and threw it upon the table.

"Don't make any mistake, Dell." he said, "About me. I don't think there's anything in the way of a haircut or a shave or a shampoo that could make me like my girl any less. But if you'll unwrap that package you may see why you had me going awhile at first."

White fingers and nimble tore at the string and paper. And then an ecstatic scream of joy; and then, alas! a quick feminine change to hysterical tears and wails, necessitating the immediate employment of all the comforting powers of the lord of the flat.

For there lay The Combs—the set of combs, side and back, that Della had worshipped long in a Broadway window. Beautiful combs, pure tortoise shell, with jeweled rims—just the shade to wear in the beautiful vanished hair. They were expensive combs, she knew, and her heart had simply craved and yearned over them without the least hope of possession. And now, they were hers, but the tresses that should have adorned the coveted adornments were gone.

But she hugged them to her bosom, and at length she was able to look up with dim eyes and a smile and say: "My hair grows so fast, Jim!"

And then Della leaped up like a little singed cat and cried, "Oh, oh!"

Jim had not yet seen his beautiful present. She held it out to him eagerly upon her open palm. The dull precious metal seemed to flash with a reflection of her bright and ardent spirit.

"Isn't it a dandy, Jim? I hunted all over town to find it. You'll have to look at the time a hundred times a day now. Give me your watch. I want to see how it looks on it."

Instead of obeying, Jim tumbled down on the couch and put his hands under the back of his head and smiled.

"Dell," said he, "let's put our Christmas presents away and keep 'em awhile. They're too nice to use just at present. I sold the watch to get the money to buy your combs. And now suppose you put the chops on."

Let us remember that the Christmas kart is a giving kart, a wide open heart that thinks of others first. The birth of the baby Jesus stands as the most significant event in all history, because it has meant the pouring into a sick world of the healing medicine of love which has transformed all manner of hearts for almost two thousand years . . . Underneath all the bulging bundles is this beating Christmas heart.

GEORGE MATTHEW ADAMS

The magi, as you know, were wise men — wonderfully wise men — who brought gifts to the Babe in the manger. They invented the art of giving Christmas presents. Being wise, their gifts were no doubt wise ones, possibly bearing the privilege of exchange in case of duplication. And here I have lamely related to you the uneventful chronicle of two foolish children in a flat who most unwisely sacrificed for each other the greatest treasures of their house. But in a last word to the wise of these days let it be said that of all who give gifts these two were the wisest. Oh all who give and receive gifts, such as they are wisest. Everywhere they are wisest. They are the magi.

TRIVIA

In France midnight services are followed by le Reveillon. Cafes and restaurants are open all night serving reveillon, which means wake up, or first call of the day. So this is a meal symbolic of a spiritual awakening to the meaning of Christ's birth. The meal can consist of oysters, sausages, wine, baked ham, roast fowl, salads, fruit, and pastries.

FOOD TRADITIONS

FRANCE

In the Paris region of France oysters are a favorite Christmas dish, followed by a cake shaped like a Yule log.

Cocktail Sauce

Serve raw oysters on the half shell set on a bed of ice, 6 at least per person. They are also nice served on the half shell on a huge brass tray with cocktails. Serve with the following cocktail sauce recipe.

Ingredients:

1/2 cup each chili sauce and ketchup, mixed
3 tablespoons horseradish
1.5 tablespoons lemon juice
2 tablespoons ground onion or chopped chives
dash of Tabasco sauce

Makes 1 Serving

Traditions

THE TRADITION OF THE NATIVITY

A popular decoration at Christmas among Christians is a manger, or creche. Whether made roughly of wood or inexpensive plastic or delicately formed of china or porcelain, populated with only the Holy Family or consisting of the Family, the Wise Men, various animals including sheep, camels, cows, horses, and birds, this is the Christian's true indication of what Christmas is: the birth of Baby Jesus. In fact, this is one of the few Christmas customs that has its root firmly in Christianity rather than in modified pagan practices.

In a very sweet, touching story, it is told that Saint Francis of Assisi first popularized the Christmas manger in 1223 AD. He wanted so much to experience the circumstances under which Christ was born that he recreated a manger scene with live people and animals, and then invited his friends to come share "his Bethlehem." According to Saint Bonaventure, writing in the thirteenth century, "That this might not be seen as an innovation, he [Saint Francis] sought and obtained license from the supreme pontiff, and they made ready a manger, and bale hay, together with an ox and an ass, he brought unto the place . . . The man of God (Saint Francis) filled with tender love, stood before the manger, bathed in tears, and overflowing with joy. Solemn masses were celebrated over the manger. Francis the Levite of Christ chanting the Holy Gospel."

After that event, creches became incredibly popular and spread over Europe, growing in opulence and involving many live players in the pageant — with the live participants dressed, strangely enough, in contemporary clothing! Soon one could also buy ornately carved sets.

Eventually, by the seventeenth and eighteenth centuries, the manger scenes had become so ornate and so elaborate that there was truly nothing of Jesus left in them.

Eventually those displays became less popular, until today they have become what they originally were: our own little Bethlehems in our own homes and churches—a reminder of the blessed birth of Christ. The living nativity now is usually in front of a church as a gift to the community—an invitation to come and remember what the season is about. And while most live nativities are not ornate, the participants must truly feel what Saint Francis felt when he wanted to experience the circumstances of the most incredible birth the world has ever known—the Gift of God come down to earth.

THE TAILOR OF GLOUCESTER

BEATRIX POTTER

In the time of swords and peri wigs and full-skirted coats with flowered lappets — when gentlemen wore ruffles, and gold-laced waistcoats of paduasoy and taffeta — there lived a tailor in Gloucester. He sat in the window of a little shop in Westgate Street, cross-legged on a table from morning till dark.

All day long while the light lasted he sewed and snipped, piecing out his satin, and pompadour, and lutestring; stuffs had strange names, and were very expensive in the days of the Tailor of Gloucester.

But although he sewed fine silk for his neighbors, he himself was very, very poor. He cut his coats without waste; according to his embroidered cloth, they were very small ends and snippets that lay about upon the table — "Too narrow breadths for nought — except waistcoats for mice," said the tailor.

One bitter cold day near Christmastime the tailor began to make a coat (a coat of cherry-colored corded silk embroidered with pansies and roses) and a cream-colored satin waistcoat for the Mayor of Gloucester.

The tailor worked and worked, and he talked to himself: "No breadth at all, and cut on the cross; it is no breadth at all; tippets for mice and ribbons for mobs! for mice!" said the Tailor of Gloucester.

When the snowflakes came down against the small leaded window-panes and shut out the light, the tailor had done his day's work; all the silk and satin lay cut out upon the table.

There were twelve pieces for the coat and four pieces for the waistcoat; and there were pocket-flaps and cuffs and buttons, all in order. For the lining of the coat there was fine yellow taffeta, and for the buttonholes of the waistcoat there was cherry-colored twist. And everything was ready to sew together in the morning, all measured and sufficient — except that there was wanting just one single skein of cherry-colored twisted silk.

Instead of being a time of unusual behavior, Christinas is perhaps the only time in the year when people can obey their natural impulses and express their true sentiments without feeling self-conscious and, perhaps, foolish. Christmas, in short, is about the only chance a man has to be himself.

FRANCIS C. FARLEY

The tailor came out of his shop at dark. No one lived there at nights but little brown mice, and THEY ran in and out without any keys!

For behind the wooden wainscots of all the old houses in Gloucester, there are little mouse staircases and secret trap-doors; and the mice run from house to house through those long, narrow passages.

But the tailor came out of his shop and shuffled home through the snow. And although it was not a big house, the tailor was so poor he only rented the kitchen.

He lived alone with his cat; it was called Simpkin.

"Miaw?" said the cat when the tailor opened the door, "miaw?"

The tailor replied: "Simpkin, we shall make our fortune, but I am worn to a raveling. Take this groat (which is our last fourpence), and, Simpkin, take a china pipkin, buy a penn'orth of bread, a penn'orth of milk, and a penn'orth of sausages. And oh, Simpkin, with the last penny of our fourpence buy me one penn'orth of cherry-colored silk. But do not lose the last penny of the fourpence, Simpkin, or I am undone and worn to a thread-paper, for I have NO MORE TWIST."

Then Simpkin again said "Miaw!" and took the groat and the pipkin, and went out into the dark.

The tailor was very tired and beginning to be ill. He sat down by the hearth and talked to himself about that wonderful coat.

"I shall make my fortune — to be cut bias — the Mayor of Gloucester is to be married on Christmas Day in the morning, and he hath ordered a coat and an embroidered waistcoat."

Then the tailor started; for suddenly, interrupting him from the dresser at the other side of the kitchen came a number of little noises. Tip tap, tip tap, tip tap tip!

FOR FUN

TOP 10 THINGS MOMS DON'T WANT TO HEAR THEIR
KIDS SAY AT CHRISTMAS
10. "Mom, I need a reindeer outfit for the pageant tomorrow."
9. "I told Santa I want a Saint Bernard. He said 'Sure.'"
8. "Don't come in the kitchen, Mom."
7. "I'm wrapping your present. I can't get him to hold still."
6. "Hey Mikey, I bet my can of spray snow shoots farther than your can."
5. "Just makin' sure Santa can get down this chimney …"
4. "I told Pastor Harold you'd direct the Christmas play.
I'm gonna be a wise guy."
3. "Bring the candle over, Jimmy. Let's see if this tree is really fireproof."
2. "Hey, Mom. How come Dad's hanging from the roof?"
1. "But I wanted the other one."

"Now what can that be?" said the Tailor of Gloucester, jumping up from his chair. The tailor crossed the kitchen, and stood quite still beside the dresser, listening, and peering through his spectacles.

"This is very peculiar," said the Tailor of Gloucester, and he lifted up the tea-cup which was upside down.

Out stepped a little live lady mouse, and made a curtsy to the tailor! Then she hopped away down off the dresser, and under the wainscot.

The tailor sat down again by the fire, warming his poor cold hands. But all at once, from the dresser, there came other little noises. Tip tap, tip tap, tip tap tip!

"This is passing extraordinary!" said the Tailor of Gloucester, and turned over another tea-cup, which was upside down.

Out stepped a little gentleman mouse, and made a bow to the tailor!

And out from under teacups and from under bowls and basins, stepped other and more little mice, who hopped away down off the dresser and under the wainscot.

The tailor sat down, close over the fire, lamenting: "One- and-twenty buttonholes of cherry-coloured silk! To be finished by noon of Saturday: and this is Tuesday evening. Was it right to let loose those mice, undoubtedly the property of Simpkin? Alack, I am undone, for I have no more twist!"

The little mice came out again and listened to the tailor; they took notice of the pattern of that wonderful coat. They whispered to one another about the taffeta lining and about little mouse tippets.

And then suddenly they all ran away together down the passage behind the wainscot, squeaking and calling to one another as they ran from house to house.

Not one mouse was left in the tailor's kitchen when Simpkin came back. He set down the pipkin of milk upon the dresser, and looked suspiciously at the tea-cups. He wanted his supper of little fat mouse!

FACTOIDS

During the Christmas buying season, Visa cards alone are used an average 5,340 time every minute in the United States.

"Simpkin," said the tailor, "where is my TWIST?"

But Simpkin hid a little parcel privately in the tea-pot, and spit and growled at the tailor; and if Simpkin had been able to talk, he would have asked: "Where is my MOUSE?"

"Alack, I am undone!" said the Tailor of Gloucester, and went sadly to bed.

All that night long Simpkin hunted and searched through the kitchen, peeping into cupboards and under the wainscot, and into the teapot where he had hidden that twist; but still he found never a mouse!

The poor old tailor was very ill with a fever, tossing and turning in his four-post bed; and still in his dreams he mumbled: "No more twist! no more twist!"

Christmas waves a magic wand over this world, and behold, everything is softer and more beautiful.
NORMAN VINCENT PEALE

What should become of the cherry-coloured coat? Who should come to sew it, when the window was barred, and the door was fast locked?

Out-of-doors the market folks went trudging through the snow to buy their geese and turkeys, and to bake their Christmas pies; but there would be no dinner for Simpkin and the poor old tailor of Gloucester.

The tailor lay ill for three days and nights; and then it was Christmas Eve, and very late at night. And still Simpkin wanted his mice, and mewed as he stood beside the four-post bed.

But it is in the old story that all the beasts can talk in the night between Christmas Eve and Christmas Day in the morning (though there are very few folk that can hear them, or know what it is that they say).

When the Cathedral clock struck twelve there was an answer — like an echo of the chimes — and Simpkin heard it, and came out of the tailor's door, and wandered about in the snow.

From all the roofs and gables and old wooden houses in Gloucester came a thousand merry voices singing the old Christmas rhymes — all the old songs that ever I heard of, and some that I don't know, like Whittington's bells.

TRIVIA

Christmas Day in Ukraine can be celebrated on either December 25, in faithful alliance with the Roman Catholic Gregorian calendar, or on January 7, which is the Orthodox or Eastern Rite (Julian calendar), the church holy day.

Under the wooden eaves the starlings and sparrows sang of Christmas pies; the jackdaws woke up in the Cathedral tower; and although it was the middle of the night the throstles and robins sang; and the air was quite full of little twittering tunes.

But it was all rather provoking to poor hungry Simpkin.

From the tailor's ship in Westgate came a glow of light; and when Simpkin crept up to peep in at the window it was full of candles.

There was a snipping of scissors, and snapping of thread; and little mouse voices sang loudly and gaily:

"Four-and-twenty tailors
Went to catch a snail.
The best man amongst them
Durst not touch her tail;

She put out her horns
Like a little kyloe cow.
Run, tailors, run!
Or she'll have you all e'en now!"

Then without a pause the little mouse voices went on again:

"Sieve my lady's oatmeal,
Grind my lady's flour,
Put it in a chestnut.
Let it stand an hour – "

"Mew! Mew!" interrupted Simpkin, and he scratched at the door. But the key was under the tailor's pillow; he could not get in.

The little mice only laughed, and tried another tune—

"Three little mice sat down to spin,
Pussy passed by and she peeped in.
What are you at, my fine little men?
Making coats for gentlemen.
Shall I come in and cut off your threads?
Oh, no, Miss Pussy, You'd bite off our heads!"

"Mew! scratch! scratch!" scuffled Simpkin on the window-sill; while the little mice inside sprang to their feet, and all began to shout all at once in little twittering voices: "No more twist! No more twist!" And they barred up the window-shutters and shut out Simpkin.

Simpkin came away from the shop and went home considering in his mind. He found the poor old tailor without fever, sleeping peacefully.

Then Simpkin went on tip-toe and took a little parcel of silk out of the tea-pot; and looked at it in the moonlight; and he felt quite ashamed of his badness compared with those good little mice!

When the tailor awoke in the morning, the first thing which he saw, upon the patchwork quilt, was a skein of cherry-coloured twisted silk, and beside his bed stood the repentant Simpkin!

The sun was shining on the snow when the tailor got up and dressed, and came out into the street with Simpkin running before him.

Christmas, children, is not date. It is a state of mind.
MARY ELLEN CHASE

"Alack," said the tailor, "I have my twist; but no more strength — nor time — than will serve to make me one single buttonhole; for this is Christmas Day in the Morning! The Mayor of Gloucester shall be married by noon — and where is his cherry-coloured coat?"

He unlocked the door of the little shop in Westgate Street, and Simpkin ran in, like a cat that expects something.

But there was no one there! Not even one little brown mouse!

But upon the table — oh joy! The tailor gave a shout — there, where he had left plain cuttings of silk there lay the most beautiful coat and embroidered satin waistcoat that ever were worn by a Mayor of Gloucester!

Everything was finished except just one single cherry-coloured buttonhole, and where that buttonhole was wanting there was pinned a scrap of paper with these words — in little teeny weeny writing — NO MORE TWIST.

And from then began the luck of the Tailor of Gloucester; he grew quite stout, and he grew quite rich.

He made the most wonderful waistcoats for all the rich merchants of Gloucester, and for all the fine gentlemen of the country round.

Never were seen such ruffles, or such embroidered cuffs and lappets! But his buttonholes were the greatest triumph of it all.

The stitches of those buttonholes were so neat — SO neat —

I wonder how they could be stitched by an old man in spectacles, with crooked old fingers, and a tailor's thimble.

The stitches of those buttonholes were so small—SO small—they looked as if they had been made by little mice!

FOR FUN

CHRISTMAS QUIZ

What did Adam say on the day before Christmas?
It's Christmas, Eve!

What does Father Christmas suffer from if he gets
stuck in a chimney?
Santa Claustrophobia!

What do you call a letter sent up the chimney on
Christmas Eve?
Black mail!

What did the guest sing at the Eskimo's Christmas
party? Freeze a jolly good fellow!

How do snowmen travel around?
By icicle!

What do snowmen eat for lunch?
Icebergers!

Christmas Around the World

BRAZIL

Papai Noel, or Father Christmas, is the gift-bringer in Brazil. According to legend, he lives in Greenland, not the North Pole. Because Christmas comes in Brazil's summertime, he wears a silk outfit, not a wool suit with ermine cuffs.

One Brazilian tradition is to create a nativity scene, or presepio. This word comes from the Hebrew *presepium*, which means the bed of straw upon which Jesus first slept. These nativity scenes are common in northeastern Brazil and are displayed in churches, homes, and stores.

Fresh flowers are common decorations. Fireworks light the skies over the cites, and huge Christmas trees made only of electric lights glow against the night skies in major cities such as Brasilia, San Paolo, and Rio de Janeiro.

Catholics attend midnight mass (Missa do Galo), which usually concludes at one o'clock on Christmas morning. Christmas dinner includes turkey, ham, rice, vegetables, and fruit dishes.

FOR FUN

Top 6 B&W Christmas Movies of All Time

Editor's Note: Do yourself a favor and view the following classics in their original black & white versions. Modern-day colorized versions don't do them justice.

6. HOLIDAY INN
(1942, Fred Astaire and Bing Crosby)

Astaire and Crosby dance their way through the seasons at a New England inn that is open only on holidays. For Christmas, Bing writes a special song, one that is to become one of the best-selling songs of all time, "White Christmas."

5. THE BELLS OF ST. MARYS
(1945, Bing Crosby and Ingrid Bergman)

Crosby re-creates his role as Father O'Malley from the award-winning Going My Way. The addition of Ingrid Bergman as a nun and Henry Travers (the angel Clarence in Its a Wonderful Life) helps to round this into a true holiday treat.

4. CHRISTMAS IN CONNECTICUT
(1945, Barbara Stanwyck)

Stanwyck plays a writer for a women's magazine who paints a picture of her serene farm where she makes gourmet meals, cares for her husband and baby, sews her own clothes, and milks her cow. Actually, she lives by herself in a small apartment in New York City and cannot even boil water — and things get interesting when she's asked to host a returning serviceman at her farm. Watching her try to flip pancakes is worth it all.

3. MIRACLE ON 34TH STREET
(1947, Edmund Gwenn and Maureen O'Hara)

When the Santa Claus in Macy's Thanksgiving Day Parade (Gwenn) announces he is the real Santa Claus, his employer (O'Hara) must decide if she has the faith to believe — not only in Santa Claus, but in anything she cannot see and feel herself. A very young Natalie Wood also stars in this classic.

2. IT'S A WONDERFUL LIFE
(1946, Jimmy Stewart and Donna Reed)

Jimmy Stewart is stuck in Bedford Falls, a small town that offers him none of the excitement he longs for. So when he encounters Clarence, an angel (second class — he doesn't have his wings yet) who stops him from committing suicide, Jimmy wishes he had never been born. He gets his wish, and sees how differently life all around him would be. One of the great films of all time.

1. A CHRISTMAS CAROL
(1951, Alistair Sim)

It seems that the Dickens classic attracts a new version (or two) every year, but we'll save you time and money by spotlighting the three best, which include this one. Many critics contend that Sims's 1951 edition is the cream of the black & white crop, and we at your friendly *Inspirational Christmas Almanac* rate it #3 of all the movie versions. (You'll find our first and second choices among the "Top 7 Color Christmas Movies" list.)

FOOD TRADITIONS

FRANCE

La Buche de Noel

La Buche de Noel is a sponge cake with a creamy filling. It is covered in chocolate to make it look like a Yule log.

INGREDIENTS:

1 pint heavy whipping cream
1/2 cup unsifted confectioner's sugar
1/2 cup unsweetened cocoa powder
1 teaspoon vanilla extract
6 egg whites
1/4 cup white sugar
6 egg yolks
1/2 cup white sugar
1/2 cup unsweetened cocoa powder
1/2 teaspoon vanilla extract
1 dash salt
confectioner's sugar for dusting

DIRECTIONS:

Use the first set of ingredients to make the filling. In a medium-size mixing bowl, combine the heavy cream, confectioner's sugar, cocoa, and vanilla. Whip until thick and stiff, refrigerate until needed. Preheat oven to 375 degrees F (190 degrees C). Line a 10 x 1 5-inch jelly roll pan with parchment paper.

Use the second set of ingredients to make the log. In a large glass or metal mixing bowl, beat egg whites until foamy.

Gradually add 1/4 sugar, continuing to beat until whites form stiff peaks. In another bowl, whip the egg yolks at high speed, while gradually adding the remaining sugar. Whip until yolks are thick and pale. Reduce speed and add the cocoa, vanilla, and salt. Fold the yolk mixture into the whites until the mixture is uniform. Spread evenly into the prepared pan.

Bake 12 to 15 minutes in the preheated oven, until the cake springs back when lightly touched.

Dust a clean dish towel with confectioner's sugar. Run a knife or spatula around the edge of the pan and turn the warm cake out onto the towel. Remove the parchment paper from the bottom of the cake. Starting at the short edge of the cake, roll the cake up with the towel. Then unroll the cake and spread the filling to within 1 inch of the edge: Use the towel to roll the cake up with the filling inside. Set onto a serving plate seam side down and refrigerate .until serving. Dust with confectioner's sugar before serving.

Makes 10 to 12 servings

THE THIEVES WHO COULDN'T HELP SNEEZING

THOMAS HARDY

Many years ago, when oak trees now past their prime were about as large as elderly gentlemen's walking sticks, there lived in Wessex a yeoman's son, whose name was Hubert. He was about fourteen years of age, and was as remarkable for his candor and lightness of heart as for his physical courage, of which, indeed, he was a little vain.

One cold Christmas Eve his father, having no other help at hand, sent him on an important errand to a small town several miles from home. He traveled on horseback, and was detained by the business till a late hour in the evening. At last, however, it was completed; he returned to the inn, the horse was saddled, and he started on his way. His journey homeward lay through the Vale of Blackmore, a fertile but somewhat lonely district, with heavy clay roads and crooked lanes. In those days, too, a great part of it was thickly wooded.

It must have been about nine o'clock when, riding along amid the over-hanging trees upon his stout-legged cob, Jerry, and singing a Christmas carol, to be in harmony with the season, Hubert fancied that he heard a noise among the boughs. This recalled to his mind that the spot he was traversing bore an evil name. Men had been waylaid there. He looked at Jerry, and wished he had been of any other color than light gray; for on this account the docile animal's form was visible even here in the dense shade. "What do I care?" he said aloud, after a few minutes of reflection. "Jerry's legs are too nimble to allow any highwayman to come near me."

"Ha! ha! indeed," was said in a deep voice; and the next moment a man darted from the thicket on his right hand, another man from the thicket on his left hand, and another from a tree-trunk a few yards ahead. Hubert's bridle was seized, he was pulled from his horse, and, although he struck out with all his might, as a brave boy would naturally do, he was overpowered. His arms were tied behind him, his legs bound tightly together, and he was thrown into the ditch. The robbers, whose faces he could now dimly perceive to be artificially blackened, at once departed, leading off the horse.

As soon as Hubert had a little recovered himself, he found that by great exertion he was able to extricate his legs from the cord; but, in spite of every endeavor, his arms remained bound as fast as before. All, therefore, that he could do was to rise to his feet and proceed on his way with his arms behind him, and trust to chance for getting them unfastened. He knew that it would be impossible to reach home on foot that night, and in such a condition; but he walked on. Owing to the confusion which this attack caused in his brain, he lost his way, and would have been inclined to lie down and rest till morning among the dead leaves had he not known the danger of sleeping without wrappers in a frost so severe.

Christmas is a necessity. There has to be at least one day of the year to remind us that were here for something else besides ourselves.

ERIC SEVAREID

So he wandered further onwards, his arms wrung and numbed by the cord which pinioned him, and his heart aching for the loss of poor Jerry, who never had been known to kick, or bite, or show a single vicious habit. He was not a little glad when he discerned through the trees a distant light. Towards this he made his way, and presently found himself in front of a large mansion with flanking wings, gables, and towers, the battlements and chimneys showing their shapes against the stars.

All was silent; but the door stood wide open, it being from this door that the light shone which had attracted him. On entering he found himself in a vast apartment arranged as a dining-hall, and brilliantly illuminated. The walls were covered with a great deal of dark wainscoting, formed into molded panels, carvings, closet-doors, and the usual fittings of a house of that kind. But what drew his attention most was the large table in the midst of the hall, upon which was spread a sumptuous supper, as yet untouched. Chairs were placed around, and it appeared as if something had occurred to interrupt the meal just at the time when all were ready to begin.

FACTOIDS
The movie How the Grinch Stole Christmas (2000) features more than 52,000 Christmas lights, about 8,200 Christmas ornaments, and nearly 2,000 candy canes.

Even had Hubert been so inclined, he could not have eaten in his helpless state, unless by dipping his mouth into the dishes, like a pig or cow. He wished first to obtain assistance; and was about to penetrate further into the house for that purpose when he heard hasty footsteps in the porch and the words, "Be quick!" uttered in the deep voice which had reached him when he was dragged from the horse. There was only just time for him to dart under the table before three men entered the dining-hall. Peeping from beneath the hanging edges of the tablecloth, he perceived that their faces, too, were blackened, which at once removed any remaining doubts he may have felt that these were the same thieves.

"Now, then," said the first—the man with the deep voice—"let us hide ourselves. They will all be back again in a minute. That was a good trick to get them out of the house, eh?"

TRIVIA

*Christmas is not widely celebrated in Scotland. Some historians
believe that Christmas is downplayed in Scotland because of the
influence of the Presbyterian Church, which considered Christmas
a "papist" or catholic event. As a result, Christmas in Scotland
tends to be somber.*

"Yes. You well imitated the cries of a man in distress," said the second.

"Excellently," said the third.

"But they will soon find out that it was a false alarm. Come, where shall we hide? It must be some place we can stay in for two or three hours, till all are in bed and asleep. Ah! I have it. Come this way! I have learnt that the further closet is not opened once in a twelve-month; it will serve our purpose exactly."

The speaker advanced into a corridor which led from the hall. Creeping a little farther forward, Hubert could discern that the closet stood at the end, facing the dining-hall. The thieves entered it, and closed the door. Hardly breathing, Hubert glided forward, to learn a little more of their intention, if possible; and, coming close, he could hear the robbers whispering about the different rooms where the jewels, plate, and other valuables of the house were kept, which they plainly meant to steal.

They had not been long in hiding when a gay chattering of ladies and gentlemen was audible on the terrace without. Hubert felt that it would not do to be caught prowling about the house, unless he wished to be taken for a robber himself; and he slipped softly back to the hall, out the door, and stood in a dark corner of the porch, where he could see everything without being himself seen. In a moment or two a whole troop of personages came gliding past him into the house. There were an elderly gentleman and lady, eight or nine young ladies, as many young men, besides half a dozen menservants and maids. The mansion had apparently been quite emptied of its occupants.

FOR FUN

Christmas is the time when people put so many bulbs on the outside of their houses, you don't know if they're celebrating the birth of Jesus or General Electric.

"Now, children and young people, we will resume our meal," said the old gentleman. "What the noise could have been I cannot understand. I never felt so certain in my life that there was a person being murdered outside my door."

Then the ladies began saying how frightened they had been, and how they had expected an adventure, and how it had ended in nothing at all.

"Wait awhile," said Hubert to himself. "You'll have adventure enough by-and-by, ladies."

It appeared that the young men and women were married sons and daughters of the old couple, who had come that day to spend Christmas with their parents.

The door was then closed, Hubert being left outside in the porch. He thought this a proper moment for asking their assistance; and, since he was unable to knock with his hands, began boldly to kick the door.

"Hullo! What disturbance are you making here?" said a footman who opened it; and, seizing Hubert by the shoulder, he pulled him into the dining-hall. "Here's a strange boy I have found making a noise in the porch, Sir Simon."

Everybody turned.

"Bring him forward," said Sir Simon, the old gentleman before mentioned. "What were you doing there, my boy?"

"Why, his arms are tied!" said one of the ladies.

"Poor fellow!" said another.

Hubert at once began to explain that he had been waylaid on his journey home, robbed of his horse, and mercilessly left in this condition by the thieves.

"Only to think of it!" exclaimed Sir Simon.

"That's a likely story," said one of the gentlemen- guests, incredulously.

"Doubtful, hey?" asked Sir Simon.

"Perhaps he's a robber himself," suggested a lady.

"There is a curiously wild, wicked look about him, certainly, now that I examine him closely," said the old mother.

Hubert blushed with shame; and, instead of continuing his story, and relating that robbers were concealed in the house, he doggedly held his tongue, and half resolved to let them find out their danger for themselves.

Christmas-that magic blanket that wraps itself about us, that something so intangible that it is like a fragrance. It may weave a spell of nostalgia. Christmas may be a day of feasting, or of prayer, but always it will be a day of remembrance- a day in which we think of everything we have ever loved.

AUGUSTA E. RUNDEL

"Well, untie him," said Sir Simon. "Come, since it is Christmas Eve, we'll treat him well. Here, my lad; sit down in that empty seat at the bottom of the table, and make as good a meal as you can. When you have had your fill we will listen to more particulars of your story."

The feast then proceeded; and Hubert, now at liberty, was not at all sorry to join in. The more they ate and drank the merrier did the company become; the wine flowed freely, the logs flared up the chimney, the ladies laughed at the gentlemen's stories; in short, all went as noisily and as happily as a Christmas gathering in old times possibly could do.

Hubert, in spite of his hurt feelings at their doubts of his honesty, could not help being warmed both in mind and in body by the good cheer, the scene, and the example of hilarity set by his neighbors. At last he laughed as heartily at their stories and repartees as the old Baronet, Sir Simon, himself. When the meal was almost over one of the sons, who had drunk a little too much wine, after the manner of men in that century, said to Hubert, "Well, my boy, how are you? Can you take a pinch of snuff?" He held out one of the snuff-boxes which were then becoming common among young and old throughout the country.

"Thank you," said Hubert, accepting a pinch.

"Tell the ladies who you are, what you are made of, and what you can do," the young man continued, slapping Hubert upon the shoulder.

"Certainly," said our hero, drawing himself up, and thinking it best to put a bold face on the matter. "I am a traveling magician."
"Indeed!"

"What shall we hear next?"

"Can you call up spirits from the vasty deep, young wizard?"

"I can conjure up a tempest in a cupboard," Hubert replied. "Ha-ha!" said the old Baronet, pleasantly rubbing his hands. "We must see this performance. Girls, don't go away: here's something to be seen."

"Not dangerous, I hope?" said the old lady.

Hubert rose from the table. "Hand me your snuff-box, please," he said to the young man who had made free with him. "And now," he continued, "without the least noise, follow me. If any of you speak it will break the spell."

They promised obedience. He entered the corridor, and, taking off his shoes, went on tiptoe to the closet door, the guests advancing in a silent group at a little distance behind him. Hubert next placed a stool in front of the door, and, by standing upon it, was tall enough to reach to the top. He then, just as noiselessly, poured all the snuff from the box along the upper edge of the door, and, with a few short puffs of breath, blew the snuff through the chink into the interior of the closet. He held up his finger to the assembly, that they might be silent.

"Dear me, what's that?" said the old lady, after a minute or two had elapsed.

A suppressed sneeze had come from inside the closet.

Hubert held up his finger again.

FACTOIDS

In 1647, the English parliament passed a law that made Christmas illegal. Festivities were banned by Puritan leader Oliver Cromwell, who considered feasting and revelry on what was supposed to be a holy day to be immoral. The ban was lifted only when the Puritans lost power in 1660.

"How very singular," whispered Sir Simon. "This is most interesting."

Hubert took advantage of the moment to gently slide the bolt of the closet door into its place. "More snuff," he said, calmly.

"More snuff," said Sir Simon. Two or three gentlemen passed their boxes, and the contents were blown in at the top of the closet. Another sneeze, not quite so well suppressed as the first, was heard; then another, which seemed to say that it would not be suppressed under any circumstances whatever. At length there arose a perfect storm of sneezes.

"Excellent, excellent for one so young!" said Sir Simon. "I am much interested in this trick of throwing the voice—called, I believe, ventriloquism."

"More snuff," said Hubert.

"More snuff," said Sir Simon. Sir Simon's man brought a large jar of the best scented Scotch

Hubert once more charged the upper chink of the closet, and blew the snuff into the interior, as before. Again he charged, and again, emptying the whole contents of the jar. The tumult of sneezes became really extraordinary to listen to—there was no cessation. It was like wind, rain, and sea battling in a hurricane.

"I believe there are men inside, and that it is no trick at all!" exclaimed Sir Simon, the truth flashing on him.

"There are," said Hubert. "They are come to rob the house; and they are the same who stole my horse."

TRIVIA

Christmas presents were known in antiquity among kings and chieftains, especially on the European continent. However, they have been common among ordinary people in Iceland only during the past 100 or so years.

The sneezes changed to spasmodic groans. One of the thieves, hearing Hubert's voice, cried, "Oh! mercy! mercy! let us out of this!"

"Where's my horse?" said Hubert.

"Tied to the tree in the hollow behind Short's Gibbet. Mercy! Mercy! Let us out, or we shall die of suffocation!"

All the Christmas guests now perceived that this was no longer sport, but serious earnest. Guns and cudgels were procured; all the men-servants were called in, and arranged in position outside the closet. At a signal Hubert withdrew the bolt, and stood on the defensive. But the three robbers, far from attacking them, were found crouching in the comer, gasping for breath. They made no resistance and, being pinioned, were placed in an outhouse till the morning.

Hubert now gave the remainder of his story to the assembled company, and was profusely thanked for the services he had rendered. Sir Simon pressed him to stay over the night, and accept the use of the best bedroom the house afforded, which had been occupied by Queen Elizabeth and King Charles successively when on their visits to this part of the country. But Hubert declined, being anxious to find his horse Jerry, and to test the truth of the robbers' statements concerning him.

Heap on more wood! - the wind is chill; but let it whistle as it will,
we'll keep our Christmas merry still.
SIR WALTER SCOTT

Several of the guests accompanied Hubert to the spot behind the gibbet, alluded to by the thieves as where Jerry was hidden. When they reached the knoll and looked over, behold! there the horse stood, uninjured, and quite unconcerned. At sight of Hubert he neighed joyfully, and nothing could exceed Hubert's gladness at finding him. He mounted, wished his friends "Good-night!" and cantered off in the direction they pointed out, reaching home safely about four o'clock in the morning.

CHRISTMAS CRAFTS AND HOMEMADE GIFTS

Snowmen Luminarias

Imagine welcoming snowmen lighting your Christmas walk.

MATERIALS LIST:

round fishbowls
white frost spray paint
orange oven-bake clay, such as Sculpey
golf tees
glass baking dish
black glass paint
paintbrush
silicone glue, such as E6000
crafting mesh
work gloves
old scissors
ruler
round can, such as an oatmeal container
ribbon
tea candle

DIRECTIONS:

1. In a well-ventilated work area, spray paint the fishbowls. Let dry.

2. To make a nose, form a carrot shape from orange clay. Push a golf tee in the wide end for extra strength. Place on a baking dish. Bake in the oven according to the manufacturer's directions. Let cool.

3. Glue a clay nose on each fishbowl. Let dry. Use glass paint to make the eyes and mouth. Paint quarter-size dots for the eyes and smaller dots for the mouth. To make a snowman winking, paint one eye closed with eyelashes in the corner.

4. To make a hat, cut an 18-inch circle from crafting mesh, while wearing work gloves. Center the mesh over the can. Form the mesh over the can, folding the edge into a brim. Tie a ribbon around the brim.

5. Put a tea candle in the luminaria. Place the hat on top of the luminaria.

Traditions

CHRISTMAS CARDS

Not surprisingly, Christmas cards are a modern addition to the Christmas season. Colorful or stark, religious, ambiguous, homey, or ultramodern—they come available for any taste, which is a contrast to the first Christmas card ever made.

The first card was made in England in 1843. Only 1,000 copies were made, and they all had the same message: A Merry Christmas and Happy New Year to You. The first American card was made about the same time in Albany. New York, and read: Christmas Greetings from Pease's Great Variety Store in the Temple of Fancy. So at that time, there wasn't very much to Christmas cards, and they weren't mass produced in any great numbers.

Louis Prang, a Bavarian-born lithographer, was about to change all of that. He moved to Boston. Massachusetts, in the 1850s and set about building a successful printing business. He invented a method of reproducing color oil painting, which he called the "chromolithograph technique." As an advertising ploy for this new color method of reproduction he created a card with the words "Merry Christmas" in full color. This definitely started something big for the lithographer. He began to produce a great variety of designs including the nativity, Santa Claus, children, flowers, and butterflies. As you can imagine, in these early days the cards were quite costly, so it was usually the wealthy who were able to buy and send them. At the height of his success in 1881, Prang was producing more than five million cards annually. Those Christmas-loving Germans were able to develop a less expensive method of reproducing cards around 1890, and cards then became available to the masses.

Today, with the advent of e-mail and e-cards and the increased cost of postage, fewer cards are being sent and received through the mail. But the history of Christmas cards is rich and colorful, and perhaps someday cards will regain the importance they once had as a personal contact from people who love you and to people you love.

Christmas Around the World

CHINA

Christian children decorate trees with colorful paper ornaments in the shapes of flowers, chains, and lanterns. Chinese Christmas trees are called Trees of Light. Santa Claus is called Dun Che Lao Ren, which means "Christmas Old Man." Children hang muslin stockings hoping that Christmas Old Man will fill them with gifts and treats.

The non-Christian Chinese call this season the Spring Festival and celebrate with many festivities that include delicious meals and paying respects to their ancestors. The children are the main focus of these celebrations — they receive new clothes and toys, eat delectable food, and watch firecracker displays.

CHRISTMAS CRAFTS AND HOMEMADE GIFTS

SPARKLING PINE CONES OR YULE LOGS

Depending on where you live, by the month of December the weather is already turning colder. For many of us, it's time to get those fireplaces ready for winter. This fun recipe will make your fireplace sparkle with color!

MATERIALS LIST:

large pinecones or small logs
wooden or crock containers
rubber gloves
cheesecloth bag or old pillowcase
newspapers
table salt
borax (from the laundry section of your market)
water

DIRECTIONS:

1. Put a pound of salt or borax and a gallon of water into the container. DO NOT MIX THE SALT AND BORAX! Salt gives you yellow flames, and borax gives you green. Wear rubber gloves to protect your hands.

2. Put a few cones at a time into the pillowcase. Dip them in the water mixture and soak them thoroughly.

3. Drain the cones and spread them out on the newspaper to dry. This may take several days! When they are completely dry put them in mesh bags or paper sacks so the air circulates. Treat small logs the same way for a Yule log.

4. The next time you build a fire in the fireplace, throw them on!

FOOD TRADITIONS

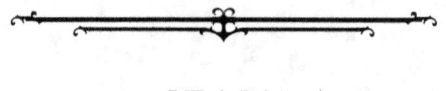

ITALY

During the Christmas holidays fanciful specialties claim a place of honor at the table. These are traditional dishes that add a festive note to seasonal menus. Typical Italian Christmas dishes include baccala (salted dried codfish), vermicelli, baked pasta, capon, and turkey. The traditional Christmas Eve dinner, which includes seven types of fish (or nine, eleven, or thirteen, depending on the town of origin), is known as La Vigilia Napoletana in southern towns and includes drowned broccoli rabe (also known as Christmas broccoli), roasted or fried eel, and caponata di pesce (fish salad) to complete the main course. The reason behind the use of fish, on the other hand, is simple: Christmas Eve is a vigilia di magro, in other words, a day of abstinence in which the Catholic Church prohibits the consumption of meat. Though this stricture is less observed now, in the past it meant that everyone would crowd the fish market on Christmas Eve.

Grilled or Fried Eel

Eel meat is oilier than that of many fish and is consequently ideally suited to the grill. This recipe is drawn from Carbla Francesconi's La Cucina Napoletana and is an indispensable part of the Neapolitan Christmas Eve dinner.

INGREDIENTS:

If you plan to grill it:
3 cloves garlic
salt
pepper
2 tablespoons olive oil
1 tablespoon vinegar
A bay leaf per piece of eel

If you plan to fry it:
all of the above, plus: flour, salt,
pot of oil for frying

DIRECTIONS:

Cut the eel into pieces about 3 inches long, wash them, dry them, and rub them with the garlic. Slip them onto skewers, alternating them with bay leaves. Season them with salt and pepper and drizzle the oil and vinegar over them; let them sit in the marinade for at least an hour.

To make grilled eel:
Grill the pieces over a medium flame for about a half hour, turning them frequently and basting them with olive oil.

To make fried eel:
Do not skewer the pieces, but rather sprinkle them with oil and dot them with pieces of bay leaf. Once they have marinated, roll the fish in flour and fry the pieces in moderately hot oil until they are browned and crunchy on the outside. Drain them well on absorbent paper and salt them.
Makes 6 servings.

FOR FUN

CAN YOU NAME THESE CHRISTMAS SONGS?

1. Oh, member of the round table with missing areas.
2. Boulder of the tinkling metal spheres.
3. Vehicular homicide was committed on Dad's mom by a precipitous darling.
4. Wanted in December: top forward incisors.
5. The apartment of two psychiatrists.
6. The lad is a diminutive percussionist.
7. Sir Lancelot with laryngitis.
8. Decorate the entryways.
9. Cup-shaped instruments fashioned of a whitish metallic element.
10. Oh, small Israel urban center.
11. Far off in a hay-bin.
12. We are Kong, Lear, and Nat Cole.
13. Duodecimal enumeration of the passage of the yuletide season.
14. Leave and broadcast from an elevation.
15. Our fervent hope is that you thoroughly enjoy your yuletide season.
16. Listen, the winged heavenly messengers are proclaiming tunefully
17. As the guardians of the woolly animals protected their charges in the dark hours
18. I beheld a trio of nautical vessels moving in this direction
19. Jubilation to the entire terrestrial globe
20. Do you perceive the same vibrations which stimulate my auditory sense organ?

ANSWERS TO CHRISTMAS SONGS:

1. *O Holy Night*
2. *Jingle Bell Rock*
3. *Grandma Got Run Over by a Reindeer*
4. *All I Want for Christmas Is My Two Front Teeth*
5. *The Nutcracker Suite*
6. *Little Drummer Boy*
7. *Silent Night*
8. *Deck the Halls*
9. *Silver Bells*
10. *O Little Town of Bethlehem*
11. *Away in a Manger*
12. *We Three Kings*
13. *The Twelve Days of Christmas*
14. *Go Tell It On the Mountain*
15. *We Wish You a Merry Christmas*
16. *Hark, the Herald Angels Sing*
17. *Shepherds Watched Their Flocks by Night*
18. *I Saw Three Ships*
19. *Joy to the World*
20. *Do You Hear What I Hear?*

Christmas Around the World

FRANCE

On Christmas Eve, children leave their shoes by the fireplace to be filled with gifts from Pere Noel, or Father Christmas. In the morning they discover that sweets, fruit, nuts, and small toys have been hung on the tree. However, in the north of France children are given gifts on December 6, which is St. Nicholas's Day. The adults give each other presents on New Year's Day.

Nearly every French home displays a creche, or nativity scene, which serves as the focus for the Christmas celebration. The creche is often peopled with little clay figures called santons, or little saints. In addition to the Holy Family, shepherds, and Magi, craftspeople also produce figurines in the form of local dignitaries and characters. The craftsmanship involved in creating these colorful santons is remarkable; some molds have been passed from generation to generation since the seventeenth century.

The Christmas tree has never been particularly popular in France, and though the use of the Yule log has faded, the French make a traditional Yule log-shaped cake called Fa Buche de Noel. The cake, among other food in great abundance, is served at le reveillon, which is a very late supper held after midnight mass on Christmas Eve. The menu for the meal varies according to regional culinary tradition. In Southern France, a log is burned in people's homes from Christmas Eve until New Year's Day. A long time ago, part of the log was used to make the wedge for good luck for the coming harvest.

CHRISTMAS CRAFTS AND HOMEMADE GIFTS

Fast-Food Toy Wreath

Decorate a wreath using small toys from fast-food restaurants.

MATERIALS LIST:

30 to 50 small toys from fast-food chains (30 to 50 does 1 wreath)
wreath
big bow to put on top or ribbon to make your own bow
twine or wire
scissors or wire cutters

DIRECTIONS:

1. Put the wreath on a table along with the toys and ribbon.
2. Cut off a piece of twine or wire long enough to go around the wreath at least once.
3. Place a toy on the wreath where you want it to be.
4. Take the wire and wrap it around the toy and the wreath and twist it.
5. Repeat for however many toys you have.
6. Put your bow on top — and ta-da!

Christmas Balls

MATERIALS LIST:

large colored glass balls
metallic paint pens
glue and glitter

DIRECTIONS:

Write family members' names on the balls with the paint pens and then use the glitter and glue to decorate. Children enjoy the personalized feel that comes with creating their own Christmas ornaments. They make great gifts for your children's teachers and friends.

CHRISTMAS BY INJUNCTION

O. HENRY

Cherokee was the civic father of Yellowhammer. Yellowhammer was a new mining town constructed mainly of canvas and undressed pine. Cherokee was a prospector. One day while his burro was eating quartz and pine burrs Cherokee turned up with his pick a nugget, weighing thirty ounces. He staked his claim and then, being a man of breadth and hospitality, sent out invitations to his friends in three States to drop in and share his luck.

Not one of the invited guests sent regrets. They rolled in from the Gila country, from Salt River, from the Pecos, from Albuquerque and Phoenix and Santa Fe, and from the camps intervening.

When a thousand citizens had arrived and taken up claims they named the town Yellowhammer, appointed a vigilance committee, and presented Cherokee with a watch-chain made of nuggets.

Three hours after the presentation ceremonies Cherokee's claim played out. He had located a pocket instead of a vein. He abandoned it and staked others one by one. Luck had kissed her hand to him. Never afterward did he turn up enough dust in Yellowhammer to pay his bar bill. But his thousand invited guests were mostly prospering, and Cherokee smiled and congratulated them.

Yellowhammer was made up of men who took off their hats to a smiling loser; so they invited Cherokee to say what he wanted.

"Me?" said Cherokee, "oh, grubstakes will be about the thing. I reckon I'll prospect along up in the Mariposas. If I strike it up there I will most certainly let you all know about the facts. I never was any hand to hold out cards on my friends."

*Christmas! The very word brings joy to our hearts. No matter how
we may dread the rush, the long Christmas lists for gifts and cards
to be bought and given-when Christmas Day comes there is still
the same warm feeling we had as children, the same warmth that
enfolds our hearts and our homes.*
JOAN WINMILL BROWN

In May Cherokee packed his burro and turned its thoughtful,
mouse-colored forehead to the north. Many citizens escorted him to
the undefined limits of Yellowhammer and bestowed upon him
shouts of commendation and farewells. Five pocket flasks without an
air bubble between contents and cork were forced upon him; and he
was bidden to consider Yellowhammer in perpetual commission for
his bed, bacon and eggs, and hot water for shaving in the event that
luck did not see fit to warm her hands by his campfire in the
Mariposas.

The name of the father of Yellowhammer was given him by the
gold hunters in accordance with their popular system of
nomenclature. It was not necessary for a citizen to exhibit his
baptismal certificate in order to acquire a cognomen. A man's name
was his personal property. For convenience in calling him up to the
bar and in designating him among other blue-shirted bipeds, a
temporary appellation, title, or epithet was conferred upon him by the
public. Personal peculiarities formed the source of the majority of
such informal baptisms. Many were easily dubbed geographically
from the regions from which they confessed to have hailed. Some
announced themselves to be "Thompsons," and "Adamses," and the
like, with a brazenness and loudness that cast a cloud upon their
titles. A few vaingloriously and shamelessly uncovered their proper
and indisputable names. This was held to be unduly arrogant, and
did not win popularity. One man who said he was Chesterton L. C.
Belmont, and proved it by letters, was given till sundown to leave the

town. Such names as "Shorty," "Bow-legs," "Texas," "Lazy Bill," "Thirsty Rogers," "Limping Riley," "The Judge," and "California Ed" were in favor. Cherokee derived his title from the fact that he claimed to have lived for a time with that tribe in the Indian Nation.

FACTOIDS

The four ghosts in Charles Dickens's A Christmas Carol were the ghosts of Christmas Past, Christmas Present, Christmas Yet to Come, and the ghost of Jacob Marley.

On the twentieth day of December Baldy, the mail rider, brought Yellowhammer a piece of news.

"What do I see in Albuquerque," said Baldy, to the patrons of the bar, "but Cherokee all embellished and festooned up like the Czar of Turkey, and lavishin' money in bulk. Him and me seen the elephant and the owl, and we had specimens of this seidlitz powder wine; and Cherokee he audits all the bills, C.O.D. His pockets looked like a pool table's after a fifteen- ball run.

"Cherokee must have struck pay ore," remarked California Ed. "Well, I'm much obliged to him for his success."

"Seems like Cherokee would ramble down to Yellowhammer and see his friends," said another, slightly aggrieved. "But that's the way. Prosperity is the finest cure there is for lost forgetfulness."

FOR FUN

Do you know what it is like to put up fifteen hundred Christmas lights on the roof of a house? The kids are giving two to one I'm gonna come down the chimney before Santa Claus does.

"You wait," said Baldy; "I'm cornin' to that. Cherokee strikes a three-foot vein up in the Mariposas that assays a trip to Europe to the ton, and he closes it out to a syndicate outfit for a hundred thousand hasty dollars in cash. Then he buys himself a baby sealskin overcoat and a red sleigh, and what do you think he takes it in his head to do next?"

"Chuck-a-luck," said Texas, whose ideas of recreation were the gamester's.

"Come and Kiss Me, Ma Honey," sang Shorty, who carried tintypes in his pocket and wore a red necktie while working on his claim.

"Bought a saloon?" suggested Thirsty Rogers.

"Cherokee took me to a room," continued Baldy, "and showed me. He's got that room full of drums and dolls and skates and bags of candy and jumping-jacks and toy lambs and whistles and such infantile truck. And what do you think he's goin' to do with them inefficacious knick-knacks? Don't surmise none— Cherokee told me. He's goin' to load 'em up in his red sleigh and—wait a minute, don't order no drinks yet—he's goin' to drive down here to Yellowhammer and give the kids, the kids of this here town, the biggest Christmas tree and the biggest cryin' doll and Little Giant Boys' Tool Chest blowout that was ever seen west of the Cape Hatteras."

Two minutes of absolute silence ticked away in the wake of Baldy's words. It was broken by the House, who, happily conceiving the moment to be ripe for extending hospitality, sent a dozen whisky glasses spinning down the bar, with the slower traveling bottle bringing up the rear.

"Didn't you tell him?" asked the miner called Trinidad.

"Well, no," answered Baldy, pensively; "I never exactly seen my way to.

"You see, Cherokee had this Christmas mess already bought and paid for; and he was all flattered up with self-esteem over his idea;

and we had in a way flew the flume with that fizzy wine I speak of; so I never let on."

"I cannot refrain from a certain amount of surprise," said the Judge, as he hung his ivory-handled cane on the bar, "that our friend Cherokee should possess such an erroneous conception of — ah — his, as it were, own town."

TRIVIA

The Super Ball was born in 1965, and it became America's most popular plaything that year. By Christmas time, only six months after it was introduced by Wham-O, seven million balls had been sold at ninety-eight cents apiece. Norman Stingley, a California chemist, invented the bouncing gray ball. In his spare time, he had compressed a synthetic rubber material under 3,500 pounds of pressure per square inch, and eventually created the remarkable ball. It had a resiliency of 92 percent, about three times that of a tennis ball, and could bounce for long periods. It was reported that presidential aide McGeorge Bundy had five dozen Super Balls shipped to the White House for the amusement of staffers.

"Oh, it ain't the eighth wonder of the terrestrial world," said Baldy. "Cherokee's been gone from Yellowhammer over seven months. Lots of things could happen in that time. How's he to know that there ain't a single kid in this town, and so far as emigration is concerned, none expected?"

"Come to think of it," remarked California Ed, "it's funny some ain't drifted in. Town ain't settled enough yet for to bring in the rubber- ring brigade, I reckon."

"To top off this Christmas-tree splurge of Cherokee's," went on Baldy, "he's goin' to give an imitation of Santa Claus. He's got a white wig and whiskers that disfigure him up exactly like the pictures of this William Cullen Longfellow in the books, and a red suit of fur-trimmed outside underwear, and eight-ounce gloves, and a stand-up, lay-down croshayed red cap. Ain't it a shame that an outfit like that can't get a chance to connect with Annie and Willie's prayer layout?"

"When does Cherokee allow to come over with his truck?" inquired Trinidad.

When we were children we were grateful to those who filled our stockings at Christmas time. Why are we not grateful to God for filling our stockings with legs?

G. K. CHESTERTON

"Mornin' before Christmas," said Baldy. "And he wants you folks to have a room fixed up and a tree hauled and ready. And such ladies to assist as can stop breathin' long enough to let it be a surprise for the kids."

The unblessed condition of Yellowhammer had been truly described. The voice of childhood had never gladdened its flimsy structures; the patter of restless little feet had never consecrated the one rugged highway between the two rows of tents and rough buildings. Later they would come. But now Yellowhammer was but a mountain camp, and nowhere in it were the roguish, expectant eyes, opening wide at dawn of the enchanting day; the eager, small hands to reach for Santa's bewildering hoard; the elated, childish voicings of the season's joy, such as the coming good things of the warm-hearted Cherokee deserved.

Of women there were five in Yellowhammer. The assayer's wife, the proprietress of the Lucky Strike Hotel, and a laundress whose washtub panned out an ounce of dust a day. These were the permanent feminines; the remaining two were the Spangler Sisters, Misses Fanchon and Erma, of the Transcontinental Comedy Company, then playing in repertoire at the (improvised) Empire Theatre. But of children there were none. Sometimes Miss Fanchon enacted with spirit and address the part of robustious childhood; but between her delineation and the visions of adolescence that the fancy offered as eligible recipients of Cherokee's holiday stores there seemed to be fixed a gulf.

Christmas would come on Thursday. On Tuesday morning Trinidad, instead of going to work, sought the Judge at the Lucky Strike Hotel.

"It'll be a disgrace to Yellowhammer," said Trinidad, "if it throws Cherokee down on his Christmas tree blowout. You might say that that man made this town. For one, I'm goin' to see what can be done to give Santa Claus a square deal."

"My co-operation," said the Judge, "would be gladly forthcoming. I am indebted to Cherokee for past favours. But, I do not see — I have heretofore regarded the absence of children rather as a luxury, but in this instance — still, I do not see — "

"Look at me," said Trinidad, "and you'll see old Ways and Means with the fur on. I'm goin' to hitch up a team and rustle a load of kids for Cherokee's Santa Claus act, if I have to rob an orphan asylum."

"Eureka!" cried the Judge, enthusiastically.

"No, you didn't," said Trinidad, decidedly. "I found it myself. I learned about that Latin word at school."

"I will accompany you," declared the Judge, waving his cane. "Perhaps such eloquence and gift of language as I possess will be of benefit in persuading our young friends to lend themselves to our project."

Within an hour Yellowhammer was acquainted with the scheme of Trinidad and the Judge, and approved it.

Citizens who knew of families with offspring within a forty-mile radius of Yellowhammer came forward and contributed their information. Trinidad made careful notes of all such, and then hastened to secure a vehicle and team.

FACTOIDS

During the Christmas/Hanukkah season, more than 1.76 billion candy canes will be made.

The first stop scheduled was at a double log-house fifteen miles out from Yellowhammer. A man opened the door at Trinidad's hail, and then came down and leaned upon the rickety gate. The doorway was filled with a close mass of youngsters, some ragged, all full of curiosity and health.

"It's this way," explained Trinidad. "We're from Yellowhammer, and we come kidnappin' in a gentle kind of a way. One of our leading citizens is stung with the Santa Claus affliction, and he's due in town tomorrow with half the folderols that's painted red and made in Germany. The youngest kid we got in Yellowhammer packs a forty-five and a safety razor. Consequently we're mighty shy on anybody to say 'Oh' and 'Ah' when we light the candles on the Christmas tree. Now, partner, if you'll loan us a few kids we guarantee to return 'em safe and sound on Christmas Day. And they'll come back loaded down with a good time and Swiss Family Robinsons and cornucopias and red drums and similar testimonials. What do you say?"

"In other words," said the Judge, "we have discovered for the first time in our embryonic but progressive little city the inconveniences of the absence of adolescence. The season of the year having approximately arrived during which it is a custom to bestow frivolous but often appreciated gifts upon the young and tender—"

"I understand," said the parent, packing his pipe with a forefinger. "I guess I needn't detain you gentlemen. Me and the old woman have got seven kids, so to speak; and, runnin' my mind over the bunch, I don't appear to hit upon none that we could spare for you to take over to your doin's. The old woman has got some popcorn candy and rag dolls hid in the clothes chest, and we allow to give Christmas a little whirl of our own in a insignificant sort of style. No, I couldn't, with any degree of avidity, seem to fall in with the idea of lettin' none of 'em go. Thank you kindly, gentlemen."

Down the slope they drove and up another foothill to the ranch-house of Wiley Wilson. Trinidad recited his appeal and the Judge boomed out his ponderous antiphony. Mrs. Wiley gathered her two rosy-cheeked youngsters close to her skirts and did not smile until she had seen Wiley laugh and shake his head. Again a refusal.

Trinidad and the Judge vainly exhausted more than half their list before twilight set in among the hills. They spent the night at a stage road hostelry, and set out again early the next morning. The wagon had not acquired a single passenger.

"It's creepin' upon my faculties," remarked Trinidad, "that borrowin' kids at Christmas is somethin' like tryin' to steal butter from a man that's got hot pancakes a-comin'."

"It is undoubtedly an indisputable fact," said the Judge, "that the, ah, family ties seem to be more coherent and assertive at that period of the year."

On the day before Christmas they drove thirty miles, making four fruitless halts and appeals. Everywhere they found "kids" at a premium.

Christmas is not just a day, an event to be observed and speedily forgotten. It is a spirit which should permeate every part of our lives.
WILLIAM PARKS

The sun was low when the wife of a section boss on a lonely railroad huddled her unavailable progeny behind her and said:

"There's a woman that's just took charge of the railroad eatin' house down at Granite Junction. I hear she's got a little boy. Maybe she might let him go."

Trinidad pulled up his mules at Granite Junction at five o'clock in the afternoon. The train had just departed with its load of fed and appeased passengers.

On the steps of the eating house they found a thin and glowering boy of ten smoking a cigarette. The dining-room had been left in chaos by the peripatetic appetites. A youngish woman reclined, exhausted, in a chair. Her face wore sharp lines of worry. She had once possessed a certain style of beauty that would never wholly leave her and would never wholly return. Trinidad set forth his mission.

"I'd count it a mercy if you'd take Bobby for a while," she said, wearily. "I'm on the go from morning till night, and I don't have time to 'tend to him. He's learning bad habits from the men. It'll be the only chance he'll have to get any Christmas."

FOR FUN

TOP 10 WORST GIFTS TO GIVE YOUR HUSBAND

10. A photo collage of your mom

9. That Giant Valu-Pak of tube socks

8. Any movie featuring Sandra Bullock other than Speed

7. The World's Greatest Polkas: The Ultimate Collection

6. Clothing you think makes him look more "up- to-date"

5. Season tickets to the ballet

4. Home Maintenance for Dummies

3. Romance for Dummies

2. The Pocket Fisherman

1. Front-row tickets for him and his best buddy for "Disney on Ice"

The men went outside and conferred with Bobby. Trinidad pictured the glories of the Christmas tree and presents in lively colors.

"And, moreover, my young friend," added the Judge, "Santa Claus himself will personally distribute the offerings that will typify the gifts conveyed by the shepherds of Bethlehem to—"

"Aw, come off," said the boy, squinting his small eyes. "I ain't no kid. There ain't any Santa Claus. It's your folks that buys toys and sneaks 'em in when you're asleep. And they make marks in the soot in the chimney with the tongs to look like Santa's sleigh tracks."

"That might be so," argued Trinidad, "but Christmas trees ain't no fairy tale. This one's goin' to look like the ten-cent store in Albuquerque, all strung up in a redwood. There's tops and drums and Noah's arks and—"

"Oh, rats!" said Bobby, wearily. "I cut them out long ago. I'd like to have a rifle—not a target one—a real one, to shoot wildcats with; but I guess you won't have any of them on your old tree."

"Well, I can't say for sure," said Trinidad diplomatically; "it might be. You go along with us and see."

The hope thus held out, though faint, won the boy's hesitating consent to go. With this solitary beneficiary for Cherokee's holiday bounty, the canvassers spun along the homeward road.

In Yellowhammer the empty storeroom had been transformed into what might have passed as the bower of an Arizona fairy. The ladies had done their work well. A tall Christmas tree, covered to the topmost branch with candles, spangles, and toys sufficient for more than a score of children, stood in the centre of the floor. Near sunset anxious eyes had begun to scan the street for the returning team of the child-providers. At noon that day Cherokee had dashed into town with his new sleigh piled high with bundles and boxes and bales of all sizes and shapes. So intent was he upon the arrangements for his altruistic plans that the dearth of children did not receive his notice. No one gave away the humiliating state of Yellowhammer, for the efforts of Trinidad and the Judge were expected to supply the deficiency.

When the sun went down Cherokee, with many wings and arch grins on his seasoned face, went into retirement with the bundle containing the Santa Claus raiment and a pack containing special and undisclosed gifts.

"When the kids are rounded up," he instructed the volunteer arrangement committee, "light up the candles on the tree and set 'em to playin' 'Pussy Wants a Corner' and 'King William.' When they get good and at it, why—old Santa'll slide in the door. I reckon there'll be plenty of gifts to go 'round."

The ladies were flitting about the tree, giving it final touches that were never final. The Spangled Sisters were there in costume as Lady Violet de Vere and Marie, the maid, in their new drama, "The Miner's Bride." The theatre did not open until nine, and they were welcome assistants of the Christmas tree committee. Every minute heads would pop out the door to look and listen for the approach of Trinidad's team. And now this became an anxious function, for night had fallen and it would soon be necessary to light the candles on the tree, and Cherokee was apt to make an irruption at any time in his Kris Kringle garb.

At length the wagon of the child "rustlers" rattled down the street to the door. The ladies, with little screams of excitement, flew to the lighting of the candles. The men of Yellowhammer passed in and out restlessly or stood about the room in embarrassed groups.

Trinidad and the Judge, bearing the marks of protracted travel, entered, conducting between them a single impish boy, who stared with sullen, pessimistic eyes at the gaudy tree.

"Where are the other children?" asked the assayer's wife, the acknowledged leader of all social functions.

"Ma'am," said Trinidad with a sigh, "prospectin' for kids at Christmas time is like huntin' in a limestone for silver. This parental business is one that I haven't no chance to comprehend. It seems that fathers and mothers are willin' for their offsprings to be drowned, stole, fed on poison oak, and et by catamounts 364 days in the year; but on Christmas Day they insists on enjoyin' the exclusive mortification of their company. This here young biped, ma'am, is all that washes out of our two days' manoeuvres."

"Oh, the sweet little boy!" cooed Miss Erma, trailing her De Vere robes to centre of stage.

FACTOIDS

For every real Christmas tree harvested, two to three seedlings are planted in its place.

"Aw, shut up," said Bobby, with a scowl. "Who's a kid? You ain't, you bet."

"Fresh brat!" breathed Miss Erma, beneath her enameled smile.

"We done the best we could," said Trinidad. "It's tough on Cherokee, but it can't be helped."

Then the door opened and Cherokee entered in the conventional dress of Saint Nick. A white rippling beard and flowing hair covered his face almost to his dark and shining eyes. Over his shoulder he carried a pack.

No one stirred as he came in. Even the Spangler Sisters ceased their coquettish poses and stared curiously at the tall figure. Bobby stood with his hands in his pockets gazing gloomily at the effeminate and childish tree. Cherokee put down his pack and looked wonderingly about the room. Perhaps he fancied that a bevy of eager children were being herded somewhere, to be loosed upon his entrance. He went up to Bobby and extended his red-mittened hand.

"Merry Christmas, little boy," said Cherokee. "Anything on the tree you want they'll get it down for you. Won't you shake hands with Santa Claus?"

"There ain't any Santa Claus," whined the boy. "You've got old false billy goat's whiskers on your face. I ain't no kid. What do I want with dolls and tin horses? The driver said you'd have a rifle, and you haven't. I want to go home."

Trinidad stepped into the breach. He shook Cherokee's hand in warm greeting.

"I'm sorry, Cherokee," he explained. "There never was a kid in Yellowhammer. We tried to rustle a bunch of 'em for your swaree, but this sardine was all we could catch. He's an atheist, and he don't believe in Santa Claus. It's a shame for you to be out all this truck. But me and the Judge was sure we could round up a wagonful of candidates for your gimcracks."

"That's all right," said Cherokee gravely. "The expense don't amount to nothin' worth mentionin'. We can dump the stuff down a shaft or throw it away. I don't know what I was thinkin' about; but it never occurred to my cogitations that there wasn't any kids in Yellowhammer."

Meanwhile the company had relaxed into a hollow but praiseworthy imitation of a pleasure gathering.

Bobby had retreated to a distant chair, and was coldly regarding the scene with ennui plastered thick upon him. Cherokee, lingering with his original idea, went over and sat beside him.

FOR FUN

A woman went to the post office to buy stamps for her Christmas cards. "What denomination?" asked the clerk.
"Oh, good heavens! Have we come to this?" said the woman.
"Well, give me 30 Catholic, 10 Baptist, 20 Lutheran, and 4 Presbyterian."

"Where do you live, little boy?" he asked respectfully.

"Granite Junction," said Bobby without emphasis.

The room was warm. Cherokee took off his cap, and then removed his beard and wig.

"Say!" exclaimed Bobby, with a show of interest, "I know your mug, all right."

"Did you ever see me before?" asked Cherokee.

"I don't know; but I've seen your picture lots of times."

"Where?"

The boy hesitated. "On the bureau at home," he answered.

"Let's have your name, if you please, buddy."

"Robert Lumsden. The picture belongs to my mother. She puts it under her pillow of nights. And once I saw her kiss it. I wouldn't. But women are that way."

TRIVIA

The world's first singing commercial aired on the radio on Christmas Eve, 1926, for Wheaties cereal. The four male singers, eventually known as the Wheaties Quartet, sang the jingle. The Wheaties Quartet, comprised of an undertaker, a bailiff, a printer, and a businessman, performed the song for the next six years, at six dollars per singer per week. The commercials were a resounding success.

Cherokee rose and beckoned to Trinidad.

"Keep this boy by you till I come back," he said. "I'm goin' to shed these Christmas duds, and hitch up my sleigh. I'm goin' to take this kid home."

"Well, infidel," said Trinidad, taking Cherokee's vacant chair,

"and so you are too superannuated and effete to yearn for such mockeries as candy and toys, it seems."

"I don't like you," said Bobby, with acrimony. "You said there would be a rifle. A fellow can't even smoke. I wish I was at home." Cherokee drove his sleigh to the door, and they lifted Bobby in beside him. The team of fine horses sprang away prancingly over the hard snow. Cherokee had on his $500 overcoat of baby sealskin. The laprobe that he drew about them was as warm as velvet.

Bobby slipped a cigarette from his pocket and was trying to snap a match.

"Throw that cigarette away," said Cherokee, in a quiet but new voice.

Bobby hesitated, and then dropped the cylinder overboard. "Throw the box, too," commanded the new voice.

More reluctantly the boy obeyed.

"Say," said Bobby, presently, "I like you. I don't know why. Nobody never made me do anything I didn't want to do before."

"Tell me, kid," said Cherokee, not using his new voice, "are you sure your mother kissed that picture that looks like me?"

"Dead sure. I seen her do it."

"Didn't you remark somethin' awhile ago about wanting a rifle?"

"You bet I did. Will you get me one?"

"Tomorrow — silver-mounted." Cherokee took out his watch. "Half-past nine. We'll hit the Junction plumb on time with Christmas Day. Are you cold? Sit closer, son."

FOOD TRADITIONS

GERMANY

Good food belongs to German Christmas celebrations as much as the Christmas tree. And many a traditional dish dates back to medieval times or even earlier. Two beverages now enjoyed around the world would include eggnog and wassail.

In earlier times, Christians would fast during the forty days between St. Martin's Day and Christmas. On the first day of Christmas, Germans broke the fast with goose. But, Christmas Eve was still a day of fasting, and so only fish, salad, bread, and vegetables would be served.

Bavarian Eggnog

INGREDIENTS:

2 tablespoons unflavored gelatin
4 cups eggnog
1 cup marshmallow cream
2 teaspoons vanilla
1/4 teaspoon almond extract
1/2 cup heavy cream, whipped

TOPPING:

2 cups canned cherry pie filling
2 tablespoons fresh lemon juice

DIRECTIONS:

Dissolve the gelatin in 2 cups of eggnog over low heat, stirring constantly. Stir in marshmallow cream to dissolve. Add remaining eggnog and flavor extract and blend well. Chill mixture 1 hour.

Whip cream and fold into chilled mixture. Pour mixture into a mold and chill until firm. Carefully remove from mold and place on platter. Serve with cherry topping. For topping, mix pie filling with the fresh lemon juice to thin a bit.

Makes 8 servings.

Christmas Around the World

GREECE

Saint Nicholas is important in Greece as the patron saint of his clothes are drenched with brine, his beard drips with seawater, and his face is covered with perspiration because he has been working hard against the waves to rescue sinking ships. Greek ships never leave port without some sort of Saint Nicholas icon on board.

At Christmas very few presents are exchanged. Instead, small gifts are given to hospitals and orphanages. Priests sometimes go from house to house sprinkling holy water to get rid of the bad spirits. Gifts are exchanged on January 1, Saint Basil's Day.

On Christmas Eve small boys go caroling to the beating of drums and the tinkling of triangles. They are given dried figs, almonds, walnuts, and lots of sweets or sometimes small gifts.

After forty days of fasting, the Christmas feast is looked forward to with anticipation. Pigs are slaughtered, and on almost every table are loaves of christopsomo, or Christ bread. This bread is made in large sweet loaves of various shapes, and the crusts are engraved and decorated in some way that reflects the family's profession.

Christmas trees are not commonly used in Greece, but when they are, the evergreen is decorated with tinsel and a star on top. In almost every home the main symbol of the season is a shallow wooden bowl with a piece of wire suspended across the rim; from which hangs a sprig of basil wrapped around a wooden cross. A small amount of water is kept in the bowl to keep the basil alive and fresh. Once a day, a family member, usually the mother, dips the cross and basil into some holy water and uses it to sprinkle water in each room of the house. This ritual is believed to keep away the kallikantzari, mischievous goblins that appear during the twelve days of Christmas.

Traditions

THE TRADITIONS OF EVERGREENS

Evergreens bring such beauty and freshness to the Christmas season that it's hard to imagine that something so steeped in our current traditions could have such pagan beginnings. But before we take a look at the paganism, let's enjoy the Christian symbolism.

From the earliest days of Christianity, the evergreen wreath has always been an emblem of eternal life and God's faithfulness to all humanity. Holly, with its green leaves, its prickly points, and its red berries, suggested that the Child born in the manger would wear a crown of thorns and shed drops of blood. Mistletoe, long associated in the pre-Christian world with healing, became a symbol of the healing power of Christ.

For us today it becomes the joyous, happy symbol of life eternal in our Lord Jesus Christ, and of the eternal love of God. The comforting green color reminds us that the new life God gives to us will never die.

Let's take a look at the ancient beginnings of the use and meanings of evergreens.

From ancient times, evergreens have symbolized life and eternity. Long before the birth of Christ, the use of evergreen branches was always a part of festive processions. In these ancient times, evil spirits were believed to roam the earth during the winter months. These were terrifying times for pagans, and they looked for protection from any source available. The always-green trees and bushes offered hope simply because they didn't die when everything else did. To these people living in such precarious times, it was strong magic that kept the plants alive.

The very origins of mistletoe have their source in magic. The Celtic word *mistel* means "dung," while *tan* means "twig." People noticed that there were usually bird droppings on the branches where the mistletoe grew. Since they also believed life could spring forth spontaneously from dung, it wasn't too much of a stretch for the people to decide that mistletoe magically came from bird droppings on a branch.

But where did the tradition of kissing beneath a sprig of mistletoe come from? Frigga, a Norse goddess, gave her son Balder a sprig of mistletoe to guard him against the elements. However, another god used an arrow made of mistletoe to kill Balder. Frigga cried tears of white berries to bring her son back to life, and promised to kiss anyone who rested beneath the plants that grew on trees from those tears. Druid priests, once again seizing an opportunity, cut the mistletoe off the oak trees with a golden sickle and gave the branches to their people with the words "all heal." The people would hang the branches in their doorways to offer the blessing of Frigga to others. Some modern Europeans still practice the custom of kissing beneath the branches of mistletoe to receive from Frigga the blessings of life, fertility, peace, and freedom from disease that she promised.

Victorians loved the idea of kissing under mistletoe and made it their own by allowing males to kiss unattached females who were lucky enough to be caught standing under the magical bough. And to observe the correct etiquette, a man should pluck a berry when he kisses a woman under the mistletoe. When the last berry is gone, there should be no more kissing!

FOR FUN

Top 7 Color Christmas Movies of All Time

7. ELF
(2003, Will Ferrell)

Ferrell is a "special" elf, taller and less talented at making toys than the true elves he lives with at the North Pole. The thing is, he is really from New York. So he leaves Santa's workshop to venture to Manhattan in search of his father, who is less than excited to learn he has a son who thinks he is an elf. Features a killer rendition of Baby, It's Cold Outside." (Rated PG for some mild crude humor.)

6. WHITE CHRISTMAS
(1954, Bing Crosby and Danny Kaye)

Twelve years after Holiday Inn, we are once again at a New England inn where Bing Crosby pairs with Danny Kaye to reprise Bing's famous song along with more great song-and-dance numbers.

5. THE SANTA CLAUSE
(1994, Tim Allen)

A delight for kids and grown-ups alike. When Scott Calvin (Allen) accidentally kills Santa on Christmas Eve, he finds himself saddled with the job. Trouble is, neither his coworkers nor his ex believe him. (Rated PG for a few crude moments).

4. NATIONAL LAMPOONS CHRISTMAS VACATION
(1989, Chevy Chase and Beverly D'Angelo)

Clark Griswold (Chase) is not the man you want putting up your Christmas lights! Anyone who has ever fantasized about having the "perfect family Christmas" will identify with Griswold as he and his wacky family celebrate Christmas with hazard and mayhem galore. (Rated PG-13 — some moments unsuitable for young children.)

3. A CHRISTMAS STORY
(1983, Peter Billingsley and Darren McGavin)

All Ralphie wants for Christmas is a real Red Ryder BB gun — but his mom insists he'll shoot his eye out. The movie answers the age-old question, If you lick a cold metal pole with your tongue, will it stick? Warm nostalgia for all who were children during the late 1940s — and delightful chuckles for everyone else.

2. SCROOGE
(1972, Albert Finney and Sir Alec Guinness)

Among the dozens of movies based on A Christmas Carol are several musical versions. None are better than Scrooge, the consummate musical version starring Albert Finney as the wonderfully irascible miser. You and your family will revel in the delightful musical score and even catch yourselves moving to the show-stopper conclusion.

1. A CHRISTMAS CAROL
(1984, George C. Scott)

This definitive version from Hallmark Hall of Fame is perhaps the most true to Dickens's original story and features a masterful interpretation by George C. Scott. Outstanding acting from all characters combined with Dickens-era settings makes this version a must-see, even a must-have.

Traditions

ORIGINATION OF ORNAMENTS

Originally, Christmas decorations were homemade paper flowers, or apples, biscuits, and sweets. The earliest decorations to be bought came from Nuremburg in Germany, a city famous for the manufacturing of toys. Lauscha in Germany is famous for its glass ornaments. In 1880, America discovered Lauscha, and F. W. Woolworth went there and bought a few glass Christmas tree ornaments. Within a day he had sold out, so the next year he bought more, and within a week they, too. had sold. The year after that he bought 200,000 Lauscha ornaments. During the First World War, ornaments from Lauscha could not be obtained, so American manufacturers began to make their own ornaments. Soon, American manufacturers developed new techniques that allowed them to turn out as many ornaments in a minute as could be made in a whole day at Lauscha.

CHRISTMAS CRAFTS AND HOMEMADE GIFTS

Electronic Season's Greetings

For friends and relatives who use e-mail, consider sending electronic Christmas cards. Many websites send e-cards for free, and they offer a wide variety of cards from which to choose. Do an internet search for other free greeting card sites.

Cookie Exchange

Contact six friends and ask each of them to make six dozen of the same kind of cookie. Meet for coffee, sample the cookies, and go home with a dozen of each kind. Give sample baskets as gifts to teachers and friends or keep them for your family through the holiday.

THE WIND IN THE WILLOWS

KENNETH GRAHAME

The sheep ran huddling together against the hurdles, blowing out thin nostrils and stamping with delicate fore-feet, their heads thrown back and a light steam rising from the crowded sheep-pen into the frosty air, as the two animals hastened by in high spirits, with much chatter and laughter. They were returning across country after a long day's outing with Otter, hunting and exploring on the wide uplands where certain streams tributary to their own River had their first small beginnings; and the shades of the short winter day were closing in on them, and they had still some distance to go. Plodding at random across the plough, they had heard the sheep and had made for them; and now, leading from the sheep-pen, they found a beaten track that made walking a lighter business, and responded, moreover, to that small inquiring something which all animals carry inside them, saying unmistakably, "Yes, quite right; this leads home!"

Christmas is for children. But it is for grown-ups too. Even if it is
a headache, a chore, and nightmare, it is a period of necessary
defrosting of chill and hide bound hearts.
LENORA MATTINGLY WEBER

"It looks as if we were coming to a village," said the Mole somewhat dubiously, slackening his pace, as the track, that had in time become a path and then had developed into a lane, now handed them over to the charge of a well-metalled road. The animals did not hold with villages, and their own highways, thickly frequented as they were, took an independent course, regardless of church, post office, or public-house.

"Oh, never mind!" said the Rat. "At this season of the year they're all safe indoors by this time, sitting round the fire; men, women, and children, dogs and cats and all. We shall slip through all right, without any bother or unpleasantness, and we can have a look at them through their windows if you like, and see what they're doing."

The rapid nightfall of mid-December had quite beset the little village as they approached it on soft feet over a first thin fall of powdery snow. Little was visible but squares of a dusky orange-red on either side of the street, where the firelight or lamplight of each cottage overflowed through the casements into the dark world without. Most of the low latticed windows were innocent of blinds, and to the lookers-in from outside, the inmates, gathered round the tea-table, absorbed in handiwork, or talking with laughter and gesture, had each that happy grace which is the last thing the skilled actor shall capture— the natural grace which goes with perfect unconsciousness of observation. Moving at will from one theatre to another, the two spectators, so far from home themselves, had something of wistfulness in their eyes as they watched a cat being stroked, a sleepy child picked up and huddled off to bed, or a tired man stretch and knock out his pipe on the end of a smoldering log.

But it was from one little window, with its blind drawn down, a mere blank transparency on the night, that the sense of home and the little curtained world within walls—the larger stressful world of outside Nature shut out and forgotten—most pulsated. Close against the white blind hung a birdcage, clearly silhouetted, every wire, perch, and appurtenance distinct and recognizable, even to yesterday's dull- edged lump of sugar. On the middle perch the fluffy occupant, head tucked well into feathers, seemed so near to them as to be easily stroked, had they tried; even the delicate tips of his plumped-out plumage penciled plainly on the illuminated screen. As they looked, the sleepy little fellow stirred uneasily, woke, shook himself, and raised his head. They could see the gape of his tiny beak as he yawned in a bored sort of way, looked round, and then settled his head into his back again, while the ruffled feathers gradually subsided into perfect stillness. Then a gust of bitter wind took them in the back of the neck, a small sting of frozen sleet on the skin woke them as from a dream, and they knew their toes to be cold and their legs tired, and their own home distant a weary way.

FOR FUN

TOP 7 WORST GIFTS TO GIVE YOUR PASTOR

7. Last year's fruitcake
6. This year's fruitcake
5. A subscription to Better Preaching magazine
4. A waterslide to liven up baptisms
3. A public-speaking manual that advises,
"Imagine your audience naked."
2. A King James Bible with a note:
Jesus and Paul used this version, so why don't we?
1. A Grumpy T-shirt from Disney World.

Once beyond the village, where the cottages ceased abruptly, on either side of the road they could smell through the darkness the friendly fields again; and they braced themselves for the last long stretch, the home stretch, the stretch that we know is bound to end, sometime, in the rattle of the door- latch, the sudden firelight, and the sight of familiar things greeting us as long-absent travelers from far over-sea. They plodded along steadily and silently, each of them thinking his own thoughts. The Mole's ran a good deal on supper, as it was pitch-dark and it was all a strange country for him as far as he knew, and he was following obediently in the wake of the Rat, leaving the guidance entirely to him. As for the Rat, he was walking a little way ahead, as his habit was, his shoulders humped, his eyes fixed on the straight grey road in front of him; so he did not notice poor Mole when suddenly the summons reached him, and took him like an electric shock.

TRIVIA

Christmas was once a moveable feast celebrated at many different times during the year. The choice of December 25 was made by Pope Julius I in the fourth century AD, because this date coincided with the pagan rituals of Winter Solstice, or Return of the Sun. The intent was to replace the pagan celebration with the Christian one.

We others, who have long lost the more subtle of the physical senses, have not even proper terms to express an animal's intercommunications with his surroundings, living or otherwise, and have only the word smell, for instance, to include the whole range of delicate thrills which murmur in the nose of the animal night and day, summoning, warning, inciting, repelling. It was one of these mysterious fairy calls from out the void that suddenly reached Mole in the darkness, making him tingle through and through with its very familiar appeal, even while yet he could not clearly remember what it was. He stopped dead in his tracks, his nose searching hither and thither in its efforts to recapture the fine filament, the telegraphic current, that had so strongly moved him. A moment, and he had caught it again; and with it this time came recollection in fullest flood.

Home! That was what they meant, those caressing appeals, those soft touches wafted through the air, those invisible little hands pulling and tugging, all one way! Why, it must be quite close by him at that moment, his old home that he had hurriedly forsaken and never sought again, that day when he first found the river! And now it was sending out its scouts and its messengers to capture him and bring him in.

Since his escape on that bright morning he had hardly given it a thought, so absorbed had he been in his new life, in all its pleasures, its surprises, its fresh and captivating experiences. Now, with a rush of old memories, how clearly it stood up before him, in the darkness! Shabby indeed, and small and poorly furnished, and yet his, the home he had made for himself, the home he had been so happy to get back to after his day's work.

And the home had been happy with him, too, evidently, and was missing him, and wanted him back, and was telling him so, through his nose, sorrowfully, reproachfully, but with no bitterness or anger; only with plaintive reminder that it was there, and wanted him.

The call was clear, the summons was plain. He must obey it instantly, and go.

"Ratty!" he called, full of joyful excitement, "hold on! Come back! I want you, quick!"

"Oh, come along, Mole, do!" replied the Rat cheerfully, still plodding along.

"Please stop, Ratty!" pleaded the poor Mole, in anguish of heart. "You don't understand! It's my home, my old home! I've just come across the smell of it, and it's close by here, really quite close. And I must go to it, I must, I must! Oh, come back, Ratty! Please, please come back!"

The Rat was by this time very far ahead, too far to hear clearly what the Mole was calling, too far to catch the sharp note of painful appeal in his voice. And he was much taken up with the weather, for he too could smell something — something suspiciously like approaching snow.

"Mole, we mustn't stop now, really!" he called back. "We'll come for it tomorrow, whatever it is you've found. But I daren't stop now — it's late, and the snow's coming on again, and I'm not sure of the way! And I want your nose, Mole, so come on quick, there's a good fellow!"

And the Rat pressed forward on his way without waiting for an answer.

Poor Mole stood alone in the road, his heart torn asunder, and a big sob gathering, gathering, somewhere low down inside him, to leap up to the surface presently, he knew, in passionate escape. But even under such a test as this his loyalty to his friend stood firm. Never for a moment did he dream of abandoning him. Meanwhile, the wafts from his old home pleaded, whispered, conjured, and finally claimed him imperiously. He dared not tarry longer within their magic circle. With a wrench that tore his very heartstrings he set his face down the road and followed submissively in the track of the Rat, while faint, thin little smells, still dogging his retreating nose, reproached him for his new friendship and his callous forgetfulness.

With an effort he caught up to the unsuspecting Rat, who began chattering cheerfully about what they would do when they got back, and how jolly a fire of logs in the parlor would be, and what a supper he meant to eat; never noticing his companion's silence and distressful state of mind. At last, however, when they had gone some considerable way further, and were passing some tree-stumps at the edge of a copse that bordered the road, he stopped and said kindly, "Look here, Mole old chap, you seem dead tired. No talk left in you, and your feet dragging like lead. We'll sit down here for a minute and rest. The snow has held off so far, and the best part of our journey is over."

The Mole subsided forlornly on a tree-stump and tried to control himself, for he felt it surely coming. The sob he had fought with so long refused to be beaten. Up and up, it forced its way to the air, and then another, and another, and others thick and fast; till poor Mole at last gave up the struggle, and cried freely and helplessly and openly, now that he knew it was all over and he had lost what he could hardly be said to have found.

The Rat, astonished and dismayed at the violence of Mole's paroxysm of grief, did not dare to speak for a while. At last he said, very quietly and sympathetically, "What is it, old fellow? Whatever can be the matter? Tell us your trouble, and let me see what I can do." Poor Mole found it difficult to get any words out between the upheavals of his chest that followed one upon another so quickly and held back speech and choked it as it came. "I know it's a — shabby, dingy little place," he sobbed forth at last, brokenly. "Not like . . . your cosy quarters . . . or Toad's beautiful hall . . . or Badger's great house . . . but it was my own little home . . . and I was fond of it . . . and I went away and forgot all about it . . . and then I smelt it suddenly . . . on the road, when I called and you wouldn't listen, Rat. And everything came back to me with a rush . . . and I wanted it! . . . O dear, O dear! . . . and when you wouldn't turn back, Ratty . . . and I had to leave it, though I was smelling it all the time . . . I thought my heart would break. We might have just gone and had one look at it, Ratty . . . only one look . . . it was close by . . . but you wouldn't turn back, Ratty, you wouldn't turn back! O dear, O dear!"

Recollection brought fresh waves of sorrow, and sobs again took full charge of him, preventing further speech.

It was always said of him, that he know how to keep Christmas well, if any man alive possessed the knowledge. May that he truly said of us, and all of us! And so, as Tiny Tim observed, "God Bless Us, Every One!"

CHARLES DICKENS

The Rat stared straight in front of him, saying nothing, only patting Mole gently on the shoulder. After a time he muttered gloomily, "I see it all now! What a pig I have been! A pig—that's me! Just a pig—a plain Pig!"

He waited till Mole's sobs became gradually less stormy and more rhythmical; he waited till at last sniffs were frequent and sobs only intermittent. Then he rose from his seat, and, remarking carelessly, "Well, now we'd really better be getting on, old chap!" set off up the road again, over the toilsome way they had come.

"Wherever are you (hic) going to (hic), Ratty?" cried the tearful Mole, looking up in alarm.

"We're going to find that home of yours, old fellow," replied the Rat pleasantly, "so you had better come along, for it will take some finding, and we shall want your nose."

"Oh, come back, Ratty, do!" cried the Mole, getting up and hurrying after him. "It's no good, I tell you! It's too late, and too dark, and the place is too far off, and the snow's coming! And—and I never meant to let you know I was feeling that way about it—it was all an accident and a mistake! And think of River Bank, and your supper!"

"Hang River Bank, and supper too!" said the Rat heartily. "I tell you, I'm going to find this place now, if I stay out all night. So cheer up, old chap, and take my arm, and we'll very soon be back there again."

Still snuffling, pleading, and reluctant, Mole suffered himself to be dragged back along the road by his imperious companion, who by a flow of cheerful talk and anecdote endeavored to beguile his spirits back and make the weary way seem shorter. When at last it seemed to the Rat that they must be nearing that part of the road where the Mole had been "held up," he said, "Now, no more talking. Business! Use your nose, and give your mind to it."

They moved on in silence for some little way, when suddenly the Rat was conscious, through his arm that was linked in Mole's, of a faint sort of electric thrill that was passing down that animal's body. Instantly he disengaged himself, fell back a pace, and waited, all attention.

The signals were coming through!

Mole stood a moment rigid, while his uplifted nose, quivering slightly, felt the air.

Then a short, quick run forward — a fault, a check, a try back — and then a slow, steady, confident advance.

The Rat, much excited, kept close to his heels as the Mole, with something of the air of a sleep-walker, crossed a dry ditch, scrambled through a hedge, and nosed his way over a field open and trackless and bare in the faint starlight.

Suddenly, without giving warning, he dived; but the Rat was on the alert, and promptly followed him down the tunnel to which his unerring nose had faithfully led him.

It was close and airless, and the earthy smell was strong, and it seemed a long time to Rat ere the passage ended and he could stand erect and stretch and shake himself. The Mole struck a match, and by its light the Rat saw that they were standing in an open space, neatly swept and sanded underfoot, and directly facing them was Mole's little front door, with Mole End painted, in Gothic lettering, over the bell-pull at the side.

Mole reached down a lantern from a nail on the wail and lit it, and the Rat, looking round him, saw that they were in a sort of fore-court.

FACTOIDS

*The custom of singing Christmas carols is very old - the earliest
English collection was published in 1521.*

A garden-seat stood on one side of the door, and on the other a roller; for the Mole, who was a tidy animal when at home, could not stand having his ground kicked up by other animals into little runs that ended in earth-heaps. On the walls hung wire baskets with ferns in them, alternating with brackets carrying plaster statuary — Garibaldi, and the infant Samuel, and Queen Victoria, and other heroes of modern Italy. Down on one side of the fore-court ran a skittle-alley, with benches along it and little wooden tables marked with rings that hinted at beer-mugs. In the middle was a small round pond containing goldfish and surrounded by a cockle-shell border. Out of the centre of the pond rose a fanciful erection clothed in more cockle-shells and topped by a large silvered glass ball that reflected everything all wrong and had a very pleasing effect.

Mole's face beamed at the sight of all these objects so dear to him, and he hurried Rat through the door, lit a lamp in the hall, and took one glance round his old home. He saw the dust lying thick on everything, saw the cheerless, deserted look of the long-neglected house, and its narrow, meager dimensions, its worn and shabby contents — and collapsed again on a hall-chair, his nose to his paws. "O Ratty!" he cried dismally, "why ever did I do it? Why did I bring you to this poor, cold little place, on a night like this, when you might have been at River Bank by this time, toasting your toes before a blazing fire, with all your own nice things about you!"

The Rat paid no heed to his doleful self-reproaches. He was running here and there, opening doors, inspecting rooms and cupboards, and lighting lamps and candles and sticking them up everywhere. "What a capital little house this is!" he called out cheerily. "So compact! So well planned! Everything here and everything in its place! We'll make a jolly night of it. The first thing we want is a good fire; I'll see to that — I always know where to find things. So this is the parlor? Splendid! Your own idea, those little sleeping-bunks in the wall? Capital! Now, I'll fetch the wood and the coals, and you get a duster, Mole — you'll find one in the drawer of the kitchen table — and try and smarten things up a bit. Bustle about, old chap!"

Encouraged by his inspiriting companion, the Mole roused himself and dusted and polished with energy and heartiness, while the Rat, running to and fro with armfuls of fuel, soon had a cheerful blaze roaring up the chimney. He hailed the Mole to come and warm himself; but Mole promptly had another fit of the blues, dropping down on a couch in dark despair and burying his face in his duster. "Rat," he moaned, "how about your supper, you poor, cold, hungry, weary animal? I've nothing to give you—nothing—not a crumb!"

"What a fellow you are for giving in!" said the Rat reproachfully. "Why, only just now I saw a sardine-opener on the kitchen dresser, quite distinctly; and everybody knows that means there are sardines about somewhere in the neighborhood. Rouse yourself! Pull yourself together, and come with me and forage."

Blessed is the season which engages the whole world
in a conspiracy of love.
HAMILTON WRIGHT MABI

They went and foraged accordingly, hunting through every cupboard and turning out every drawer. The result was not so very depressing after all, though of course it might have been better; a tin of sardines—a box of captain's biscuits, nearly full—and a German sausage encased in silver paper.

"There's a banquet for you!" observed the Rat, as he arranged the table. "I know some animals who would give their ears to be sitting down to supper with us tonight!"

"No bread!" groaned the Mole dolorously. "No butter, no—"

"No pate de foie gras, no champagne!" continued the Rat, grinning. "And that reminds me—what's that little door at the end of the passage? Your cellar, of course! Every luxury in this house! Just you wait a minute."

He made for the cellar-door, and presently reappeared, somewhat dusty, with a bottle of beer in each paw and another under each arm. "Self-indulgent beggar you seem to be, Mole," he observed. "Deny yourself nothing. This is really the jolliest little place I ever was in. Now, wherever did you pick up those prints? Make the place look so home-like, they do. No wonder you're so fond of it, Mole. Tell us all about it, and how you came to make it what it is."

Then, while the Rat busied himself fetching plates, and knives and forks, and mustard which he mixed in an egg-cup, the Mole, his bosom still heaving with the stress of his recent emotion, related— somewhat shyly at first, but with more freedom as he warmed to his subject—how this was planned, and how that was thought out, and how this was got through a windfall from an aunt, and that was a wonderful find and a bargain, and this other thing was bought out of laborious savings and a certain amount of "going without." His spirits finally quite restored, he must needs go and caress his possessions, and take a lamp and show off their points to his visitor and expatiate on them, quite forgetful of the supper they both so much needed; Rat, who was desperately hungry but strove to conceal it, nodding seriously, examining with a puckered brow, and saying, "wonderful," and "most remarkable," at intervals, when the chance for an observation was given him.

TRIVIA

Cultured Christmas trees must be shaped as they grow to produce fuller foliage. To slow the upward growth and to encourage branching, they are hand-clipped each spring. Trees grown in the wild have sparser branches and are known in the industry as "Charlie Brown" trees.

At last the Rat succeeded in decoying him to the table, and had just got seriously to work with the sardine-opener when sounds were heard from the fore-court without—sounds like the scuffling of small feet in the gravel and a confused murmur of tiny voices, while broken sentences reached them, "Now, all in a line—hold the lantern up a bit, Tommy. Clear your throats first—no coughing after I say one, two, three. Where's young Bill? Here, come on, do, we're all a-waiting—"

"What's up?" inquired the Rat, pausing in his labors.

"I think it must be the field-mice," replied the Mole, with a touch of pride in his manner. "They go round carol-singing regularly at this time of the year. They're quite an institution in these parts. And they never pass me over—they come to Mole End last of all; and I used to give them hot drinks, and supper too sometimes, when I could afford it. It will be like old times to hear them again."

"Let's have a look at them!" cried the Rat, jumping up and running to the door.

It was a pretty sight, and a seasonable one, that met their eyes when they flung the door open. In the fore-court, lit by the dim rays of a horn lantern, some eight or ten little field-mice stood in a semicircle, red worsted comforters round their throats, their fore-paws thrust deep into their pockets, their feet jigging for warmth. With bright beady eyes they glanced shyly at each other, sniggering a little, sniffing and applying coat-sleeves a good deal. As the door opened, one of the elder ones that carried the lantern was just saying, "Now then, one, two, three!" and forthwith their shrill little voices uprose on the air, singing one of the old-time carols that their forefathers composed in fields that were fallow and held by frost, or when snow-bound in chimney corners, and handed down to be sung in the miry street to lamp-lit windows at Yule-time.

> *Villagers all, this frosty tide,*
> *Let your doors swing open wide,*
> *Though wind may follow, and snow beside,*
> *Yet draw us in by your fire to bide;*
> *Joy shall be yours in the morning!*

> *Here we stand in the cold and the sleet,*
> *Blowing lingers and stamping feet,*
> *Come from far away you to greet—*
> *You by the fire and we in the street—*
> *Bidding you joy in the morning!*

For ere one half of the night was gone,
Sudden a star has led us on,
Raining bliss and benison —
Bliss tomorrow and more anon,
Joy for every morning!

Goodman Joseph toiled through the snow —
Saw the star o'er a stable low;
Mary she might not further go —
Welcome thatch, and litter below!
Joy was hers in the morning!

And then they heard the angels tell
'Who were the first to cry Nowell?
Animals all, as it befell.
In the stable where they did dwell!
Joy shall be theirs in the morning!'

The voices ceased, the singers, bashful but smiling, exchanged sidelong glances, and silence succeeded—but for a moment only. Then, from up above and far away, down the tunnel they had so lately traveled was borne to their ears in a faint musical hum the sound of distant bells ringing a joyful and clangorous peal.

"Very well sung, boys!" cried the Rat heartily. "And now come along in, all of you, and warm yourselves by the fire, and have something hot!"

"Yes, come along, field-mice," cried the Mole eagerly. "This is quite like old times!

Shut the door after you.

Pull up that settle to the fire. Now, you just wait a minute, while we—O, Ratty!" he cried in despair, plumping down on a seat, with tears impending. "Whatever are we doing? We've nothing to give them!"

"You leave all that to me," said the masterful Rat. "Here, you with the lantern! Come over this way. I want to talk to you. Now, tell me, are there any shops open at this hour of the night?"

"Why, certainly, sir," replied the field-mouse respectfully. "At this time of the year our shops keep open to all sorts of hours."

"Then look here!" said the Rat. "You go off at once, you and your lantern, and you get me—"

Here much muttered conversation ensued, and the Mole only heard bits of it, such as, "Fresh, mind! No, a pound of that will do—see you get Buggins's, for I won't have any other—no, only the best—if you can't get it there, try somewhere else—yes, of course, home-made, no tinned stuff—well then, do the best you can!" Finally, there was a chink of coin passing from paw to paw, the field- mouse was provided with an ample basket for his purchases, and off he hurried, he and his lantern.

The rest of the field-mice, perched in a row on the settle, their small legs swinging, gave themselves up to enjoyment of the fire, and toasted their chilblains till they tingled; while the Mole, failing to draw them into easy conversation, plunged into family history and made each of them recite the names of his numerous brothers, who were too young, it appeared, to be allowed to go out a- caroling this year, but looked forward very shortly to winning the parental consent.

The Rat, meanwhile, was busy examining the label on one of the beer-bottles. "I perceive this to be Old Burton," he remarked approvingly. "Sensible Mole! The very thing! Now we shall be able to mull some ale! Get the things ready, Mole, while I draw the corks."

It did not take long to prepare the brew and thrust the tin heater well into the red heart of the fire; and soon every field-mouse was sipping and coughing and choking (for a little mulled ale goes a long way) and wiping his eyes and laughing and forgetting he had ever been cold in all his life.

"They act plays too, these fellows," the Mole explained to the Rat. "Make them up all by themselves, and act them afterwards. And very well they do it, too! They gave us a capital one last year, about a field-mouse who was captured at sea by a Barbary corsair, and made to row in a galley; and when he escaped and got home again, his lady-love had gone into a convent. Here, you! You were in it, I remember. Get up and recite a bit."

The field-mouse addressed got up on his legs, giggled shyly, looked round the room, and remained absolutely tongue-tied. His comrades cheered him on, Mole coaxed and encouraged him, and the Rat went so far as to take him by the shoulders and shake him; but nothing could overcome his stage fright. They were all busily engaged on him like watermen applying the Royal Humane Society's regulations to a case of long submersion, when the latch clicked, the door opened, and the field-mouse with the lantern reappeared, staggering under the weight of his basket.

There was no more talk of play-acting once the very real and solid contents of the basket had been tumbled out on the table. Under the generalship of Rat, everybody was set to do something or to fetch something. In a very few minutes supper was ready, and Mole, as he took the head of the table in a sort of a dream, saw a lately barren board set thick with savory comforts; saw his little friends' faces brighten and beam as they fell to without delay; and then let himself loose — for he was famished indeed — on the provender so magically provided, thinking what a happy home-coming this had turned out, after all. As they ate, they talked of old times, and the field-mice gave him the local gossip up to date, and answered as well as they could the hundred questions he had to ask them. The Rat said little or nothing, only taking care that each guest had what he wanted, and plenty of it, and that Mole had no trouble or anxiety about anything.

They clattered off at last, very grateful and showering wishes of the season, with their jacket pockets stuffed with remembrances for the small brothers and sisters at home. When the door had closed on the last of them and the chink of the lanterns had died away, Mole and Rat kicked the fire up, drew their chairs in, brewed themselves a last nightcap of mulled ale, and discussed the events of the long day.

At last the Rat, with a tremendous yawn, said, "Mole, old chap, I'm ready to drop. Sleepy is simply not the word. That your own bunk over on that side? Very well, then, I'll take this. What a ripping little house this is! Everything so handy!"

He clambered into his bunk and rolled himself well up in the blankets, and slumber gathered him forthwith, as a swathe of barley is folded into the arms of the reaping machine.

The weary Mole also was glad to turn in without delay, and soon had his head on his pillow, in great joy and contentment. But ere he closed his eyes he let them wander round his old room, mellow in the glow of the firelight that played or rested on familiar and friendly things which had long been unconsciously a part of him, and now smilingly received him back, without rancor. He was now in just the frame of mind that the tactful Rat had quietly worked to bring about in him. He saw clearly how plain and simple—how narrow, even—it all was; but clearly, too, how much it all meant to him, and the special value of some such anchorage in one's existence. He did not at all want to abandon the new life and its splendid spaces, to turn his back on sun and air and all they offered him and creep home and stay there; the upper world was all too strong, it called to him still, even down there, and he knew he must return to the larger stage. But it was good to think he had this to come back to; this place which was all his own, these things which were so glad to see him again and could always be counted upon for the same simple welcome.

FACTOIDS

Hallmark introduced its first Christmas cards in 1915, five years after the founding of the company.

FOR FUN

MISTLETOE AT THE AIRPORT

It was slightly before Christmas.

The trip went reasonably well, and he was ready to go back. The airport on the other end had turned a tacky red and green, and loudspeakers blared annoying elevator renditions of cherished Christmas carols. Being someone who took Christmas very seriously, and being slightly tired, he was not in a particularly good mood.

Going to check in his luggage (which, for some reason, had become one suitcase with entirely new clothes), he saw hanging mistletoe. Not real mistletoe, but very cheap plastic with red paint on some of the rounder parts and green paint on some of the flatter and pointier parts, that could be taken for mistletoe only in a very Picasso sort of way.

With a considerable degree of irritation and nowhere else to vent it, he said to the attendant, "Even if I were not married, I would not want to kiss you under such a ghastly mockery of mistletoe."

"Sir, look more closely at where the mistletoe is."

(pause)

"Ok, I see that it's above the luggage scale, which is the place you'd have to step forward for a kiss."

"That's not why it's there."

(pause)

"Ok, I give up. Why is it there?"

"It's there so you can kiss your luggage good-bye."

FOOD TRADITIONS

GERMANY

Karpfen Blau (Blue Carp)

INGREDIENTS:

1 carp (3 to 5 pounds)
1 tablespoon salt
1/2 cup vinegar
1/2 cup white wine
1.5 cup water
1 onion
1 laurel leaf
1 tablespoon pepper
1/2 lemon
1 tablespoon butter

GARNISH:

1 tomato
1/2 lemon
1 tablespoon horseradish

DIRECTIONS:

"Blue Carp" is one of the traditional Christmas and New Year's dishes in Germany. To achieve the blue color of the fish, it is important not to scale it. The combination of the scales of the fish skin with the vinegar causes the blue coloration.

If your fish is not cleaned when you buy it, carefully cut the underside and clean it. Salt the inside of the fish.

Place fish in a bowl. Heat the vinegar to a boil and pour over the fish. Then lay the carp onto a platter, saving the vinegar.

Heat wine, water, and vinegar in a large pot. Peel onion and cut in half, Add the fish, as well as the laurel leaf, pepper, and lemon. Put on low heat and let simmer for 20 minutes. Take out the carp and lay onto a preheated platter.

Melt butter and serve separately. Cut tomatoes in slices and garnish the carp with it. Fill the lemon half with the horseradish and lay on plate.

You may serve cooked potatoes with this dish.

Traditions

CHRISTMAS GIFT GIVING

Can you imagine Christmas without gifts? We all remember that the wise men brought gifts to Jesus when he was born—gold, frankincense, and myrrh—symbolic of tribute, worship, and death (Matthew 2:1). But is that the reason we exchange gifts today? Let's see what history reveals.

Gift giving was traditional with the ancient Romans. Meg Crager, author of The Whale Christinas Catalog, wrote of this period, "Everyone gave gifts: children gave to their teachers, slaves gave to their masters, and the people gave to their Emperor." During Saturnalia (also called Kalends), the day of the new moon, the first day of the month, and the first day of the new year. Romans gave each other gifts of small candles, evergreens, lamps, incense, clay figures, fruit, and cakes.

From these early traditions of giving we can see the beginnings of our own gift-giving patterns. It's easy to see that today's much-maligned fruitcake goes back to ancient times, but it is not true—at least there is no hard evidence—that we are still passing along the same fruit and cakes that the ancient Romans used! And the highly-prized clay figures given by the Romans as substitutes for human sacrifices were the precursors to the dolls that are still a favorite gift at Christmas.

Early Christians did not practice gift giving because they did not want their religion to be associated with pagan festivals or practices.

It was much later—during the Middle Ages—that Christians began giving gifts during their Christmas celebrations. Kings demanded gifts from their subjects, and commoners began exchanging gifts with each other. December 6 was named Saint Nicholas's Day and was the traditional gift-giving time for children.

Giving gifts for the New Year was traditional for the English and French, but it was the early Dutch settlers who are responsible for bringing gift giving at Christmas to America, along with the tradition of St. Nicholas. The combined traditions of the Germans and Dutch settlers became the recognized tradition. Historically, New York has the closest association with Christmas giving. The large number of artists and writers located in New York are responsible for this as they have used the Christmas season and the always intriguing Santa for many of their writings and art.

The cost of Christmas now is absolutely staggering. In 1999 shoppers spent an astronomical $186 billion for gifts. This was also the first year in America that retailers actually began to prepare for Christmas before Halloween. In 2000 Neiman Marcus was selling their Christmas decorations in the middle of September. It seems that greed and the need to spend on extremely lavish gifts is a new and totally modern aspect of Christmas. Each year more is spent than the year before, and many retailers now depend on the Christmas buying season to pull them up into tire black financially.

CHRISTMAS CRAFTS AND HOMEMADE GIFTS

INEXPENSIVE WAYS TO CELEBRATE

Make Your Own Stocking Stuffers

Batteries: Instead of wrapping up the batteries with the gift, separate them into stocking stuffers. Since you'd need to purchase them anyway for the toys, they aren't an extra expense. By separating them out, you make a start on your stocking stuffing, and the kids will love them because they can start playing any electronic devices they received.

Disposable Camera: With all the activity going on during Christmas, you probably don't have the time to take pictures and document the day. Let your children do it for you. They'll have great fun taking photos from their own unique perspective that will add to any photo album.

Art and Craft Supplies: Again, these are supplies that you are likely to need for other activities in the future. Kids love to create, and any arts and crafts materials make great stocking stuffers. Coloring books, crayons, colored pencils, markers, and paints all fit the bill and can be used for other activities long after Christmas is over.

Travel Games: Travel-size editions of children's favorite games or card games that can be played in the car are another good stocking stuffer. The kids can play these on their own, but they have the multiple benefit that they can be used in the car to keep the children occupied during any holiday trips you make.

Christmas Encouragement: Write a Christmas letter to your child telling him or her all the fun things you remember from the past year. This doesn't cost any money, can become a lovely Christmas tradition, and will be a gift that the child will treasure long after Christmas is over.

CHRISTMAS AROUND THE WORLD

EGYPT

The Coptic Church is an Orthodox Church in which Christmas is celebrated on January 7. Advent is observed for more than a month prior, during which people are expected to fast, eating no meat, poultry, or dairy products. However, some people fast only during the last week of Advent.

On Christmas Eve, Christians go to church wearing a completely new outfit. The Christmas service ends at midnight with the ringing of church bells. Afterward, attendees go home to eat a special Christmas meal known as *fata*, which consists of bread, rice, garlic, and boiled meat.

Egyptian Christians have the day off, so on Christmas morning, they visit friends and neighbors. They take with them *kaik*, which is a type of shortbread.

CHRISTMAS CRAFTS AND HOMEMADE GIFTS

INEXPENSIVE WAYS TO CELEBRATE

Plan Family Activities

Explore ways your family can enjoy quality time together without spending money. Check your community calendars in the newspaper or online for free church programs, musicals, or community events. Caroling and trips to see Christmas lights can make special memories for you and your family.

Create Your Own Coupons

Put together coupon books as gifts for your children that will give them unique household privileges. Coupons for "One Saturday morning activity of your choice with Mom," "Stay up one hour past your bedtime," or "One free day from grounding" can prove to be big hits with your children. Coupons for friends and family might include "Dinner at my house," "One free night of babysitting," or "Two hours of yard work."

FOOD TRADITIONS

BRAZIL

Ceia de Natal is the typical Brazilian Christmas turkey marinated in Cachaca, or light rum, with onions, garlic, tomatoes, lime juice, and other spices. Should you not want to use the traditional Latino rum (Cachaca) for your marinade, the bird can also be placed in chilmole, a dark, spicy sauce, and common as a festival dish around Latin America. Stuffing fans can feast on giblet and smoked oyster stuffing made out of farofa, apricots, raisins, hard-boiled eggs, and more.

To keep with Latin tradition, rice should be part of the feast, mixed with pumpkin seeds so reminiscent of the fall season. For dinner greens, Latinos depend on kale as a staple, so Couve a Mineira (Brazilian-style kale) will satisfy this desire. Last but most important, every Latin meal should include the chile heat factor, achieved with Molho Apimentado, a hot sauce that can be sprinkled on everything and anything. It is traditionally made with malagueta peppers or green bird chiles. Malagueta peppers, Capsicum frutescens, are cousins to the tabasco chile and are truly the most distinctive spicy characteristic of Brazilian cooking. While they are difficult to find in North American markets, it is possible to find them on the Internet. If not, any small, hot chiles may be substituted. Finally, once the feast is prepared don't forget to garnish the table with poinsettia, named after the former United States ambassador to Mexico, Joel Roberto Poinsett. The flower was discovered in Mexico and has become the symbol of Christmas throughout the world, but its roots remain in Latin America. And remember, if you learn anything from celebrating Christmas Latino-style, it's that family comes first.

Ceia de Natal
(Brazilian Christmas Turkey)

Note: This recipe requires advance preparation.

The marinade suggested in this recipe is indigenous to Brazil in that it utilizes one of Brazil's great ingredients, Cachaya, made famous around the world in the sweet taste of the Caipirinha, one of Latin America's most popular alcoholic beverages. Balanced with the tart taste of lime juice and zest, this marinade is versatile and is the first step to making your holiday turkey.

INGREDIENTS:

One 12-pound turkey

MARINADE:

2 cups Cachaca or light rum
2 medium onions, diced
6 cloves garlic, chopped
4 ripe tomatoes, diced
1 cup olive oil
2 bay leaves
1 cup fresh lime juice
1/4 cup grated lime zest
2 cups water
1/2 cup chopped scallions
1 cup chopped parsley

DIRECTIONS:

In a large howl, combine all the marinade ingredients and mix well.

Place a 12-pound turkey in a roasting bag and cover it with the marinade. Close the bag so that it has no air pockets, and let the turkey marinate overnight in the refrigerator.

Giblet and Smoked Oyster Stuffing

This stuffing runs the gamut of the five food groups, relying on fruits, vegetables, protein, grains, and dairy to create the fine mixture roasting within the turkey's cavity. Farofa (cassava flour), the Latin version of corn flakes, brings it all together and gives the recipe the cohesive texture that it requires.

INGREDIENTS:

turkey giblets and neck
1 onion, diced
1 cup butter
2 cups farofa (available in Latin markets) or plain com flakes
6 fresh apricots, pits removed, diced, or 10 dry apricots rehydrated in water and diced
1/2 cup golden raisins soaked in 1 cup simple syrup and 1/4 cup dark rum
1 scallion, chopped
2 tablespoons chopped parsley
4 hard-boiled eggs, chopped
15 freshly smoked oysters, or substitute 20 canned oysters, coarsely chopped

DIRECTIONS:

In a pot, cook the giblets and neck of the turkey in water until tender, i, then dice. Reserve the cooking liquid.

In a sauté pan, cook the onion in butter until it is translucent. Add the giblets, apricots, raisins, farofa or cornflakes, and lightly cook ingredients in the butter. Slowly add the giblet stock until the mixture is moist but not too wet. Add the scallion, parsley, eggs, and oysters, and season with salt and pepper. Let cool.

TO ASSEMBLE AND COOK:

Remove the turkey from the marinade and pat dry with paper towels. Season the turkey with salt and pepper then rub with olive oil. Stuff the bird with the dressing and tie and truss the turkey. Roast in a 325 F° oven until the juice from the thigh runs clear, about 4 hours, or until the internal temperature in the thigh reaches 160 degrees F. Carve the turkey and sprinkle the slices and the stuffing with the hot sauce. Garnish with sliced carambola (star fruit).

Makes 8 servings.

FOR FUN

Christmas Tongue Twisters

Seven Santas sang silly songs.

Sarah skis super slow.

Running reindeer romp round red wreaths.

Pretty packages perfectly packed in paper.

Tiny Tim trims the tall tree with tinsel.

Santa stuffs six striped stockings.

Kris Kringle crunches candy canes.

Clever Carol carries crimson candles carefully.

Short shoppers shop for soft, short shirts.

Santa's sleigh slides on slick snow.

Candy cane cookies keep kids coming.

Comet cuddles cute Christmas kittens carefully.

OUR CHRISTMAS MEMORIES AND TRADITIONS

A MEMORABLE YEAR _____

MEMORIES OF THE PAST YEAR

WE GATHERED FOR THE HOLIDAYS AT

TRADITIONS AND SPECIAL EVENTS

_____
_____
_____
_____
_____
_____
_____
_____
_____
_____
_____
_____
_____
_____
_____

THOSE WHO JOINED IN THE CELEBRATIONS

_____
_____
_____
_____
_____
_____
_____
_____

OUR CHRISTMAS MEMORIES AND TRADITIONS

A MEMORABLE YEAR _____

MEMORIES OF THE PAST YEAR

_____

_____

_____

_____

_____

_____

_____

_____

_____

WE GATHERED FOR THE HOLIDAYS AT

_____

_____

_____

_____

_____

TRADITIONS AND SPECIAL EVENTS

_____
_____
_____
_____
_____
_____
_____
_____
_____
_____
_____
_____
_____
_____
_____

THOSE WHO JOINED IN THE CELEBRATIONS

_____
_____
_____
_____
_____
_____
_____

OUR CHRISTMAS MEMORIES
AND TRADITIONS

A MEMORABLE YEAR _____

MEMORIES OF THE PAST YEAR

_____
_____
_____
_____
_____
_____
_____
_____
_____
_____

WE GATHERED FOR THE HOLIDAYS AT

_____
_____
_____
_____

TRADITIONS AND SPECIAL EVENTS

_____

_____

_____

_____

_____

_____

_____

_____

_____

_____

_____

_____

_____

_____

THOSE WHO JOINED IN THE CELEBRATIONS

_____

_____

_____

_____

_____

_____

_____

OUR CHRISTMAS MEMORIES AND TRADITIONS

A MEMORABLE YEAR _____

MEMORIES OF THE PAST YEAR

_____

_____

_____

_____

_____

_____

_____

_____

_____

_____

WE GATHERED FOR THE HOLIDAYS AT

_____

_____

_____

_____

_____

TRADITIONS AND SPECIAL EVENTS

_____

_____

_____

_____

_____

_____

_____

_____

_____

_____

_____

_____

_____

_____

_____

THOSE WHO JOINED IN THE CELEBRATIONS

_____

_____

_____

_____

_____

_____

_____

SECTION 2

Poems, Carols, and Readings

A CHRISTMAS CAROL

CHRISTINA ROSSETTI

In the bleak mid-winter
Frosty wind made moan,
Earth stood hard as iron,
Water like a stone;
Snow had fallen, snow on snow,
Snow on snow,
In the bleak mid-winter,
Long ago.

Our God, Heaven cannot hold him
Nor earth sustain;
Heaven and earth shall flee away
When He comes to reign:
In the bleak mid-winter
A stable-place sufficed
The Lord God Almighty,
Jesus Christ.

A CHRISTMAS PRAYER

Loving Father, help us remember the birth of Jesus, that we may share in the song of the angels, the gladness of the shepherds, and worship of the wise men. Close the door of hate and open the door of love all over the world. Let kindness come with every gift and good desires with every greeting. Deliver us from evil by the blessing which Christ brings, and teach us to be merry with clean hearts. May the Christmas morning make us happy to be Thy children, and Christmas evening bring us to our beds with grateful thoughts, forgiving and forgiven, for Jesus' sake.
Amen!

ROBERT LOUIS STEVENSON

Christmas Around the World

GREAT BRITAIN

In Great Britain, Father Christmas came into being after the Reformation in the 1500s. Protestants didn't believe in saints, particularly those strongly associated with Catholicism. So, they created a new Christmas figure—Father Christmas—to take the place of Saint Nicholas.

Children write letters to Father Christmas and then throw them into the fireplace so they will float up the chimney and fly to the North Pole. If the lists catch fire first, the children have to rewrite them. On Christmas Eve, youngsters hang their stockings on the ends of their beds or by the chimney so that when Father Christmas comes he can leave them something.

On Christmas morning the family opens presents and prepares for a big feast, which typically is served just after midday. At every place setting is a cracker. The meal begins with a toast, followed by the popping of the crackers. At Christmas dinner, a plum pudding is served with little treasures hidden inside that are said to bring their finders good luck.

In the afternoon, people exchange visits with neighbors and family members. Some churches in Great Britain have a Christingle service on the fourth Sunday of Advent. This is a carol service of Scandinavian origin at which every child receives an orange and a candle wrapped in a red ribbon. The candle represents Jesus, and the ribbon stands for the blood of Christ and the love of God embracing the world.

FOOD TRADITIONS

GERMANY

Bratapfel (Baked Apples)

Baked apples are ideal for cold winter evenings, and they are easily prepared.

INGREDIENTS:

4 apples (Jonathan, Boskop, or Cox Orange are best suited)
cinnamon
syrup or honey

DIRECTIONS:

Wash the apples, core them, and place them on a greased baking sheet or in a greased baking pan.

Bake apples in the oven at 350° F for approximately 30 minutes or until tender, depending on the size. Sprinkle with cinnamon, syrup, or honey.

Origins of the Christmas Carol

The word carol has roots in several languages: the Middle English *carole*, which was a kind of round dance with singing; Old French car-ole; probably from Late Latin *choraula*, meaning "choral song"; Latin *choraules*, meaning "accompanist"; Greek *khoraules* and *khoros*, meaning "choral dance." Today we simply think of carols as songs of Christmas.

The singing of carols originated in Europe. The songs, however, weren't about Christmas. Rather they were pagan tunes sung at the Winter Solstice celebration. (The Winter Solstice is the shortest day of the year, usually around the 22nd of December.) Early carols were, like the midwinter festival itself, celebratory and fun at a time when there was very little to laugh about.

Early Christians replaced the solstice celebrations with Christmas, and songs to pagan gods with worship songs to God. The earliest carols were written in Latin, a language the average person couldn't understand, so they were only sung by priests in the church.

In 1223, Saint Francis of Assisi started Nativity plays in Italy. The people in the plays sang songs in the common language that told the story of Christ's birth. Thus the people watching could enjoy and understand them.

As troubadours and minstrels began singing these types of songs, the carols spread to France, Spain, Germany, and other European countries. These traveling singers would often change the words for the local people. By the end of the Middle Ages, common folks were singing carols even in churches.

The Christian church took a very dim view of these carols and strongly discouraged their use. In 1290 the Council at Avignon actually banned the singing of carols, but this had little effect on the common people who loved the old tunes.

In the fifteenth century the church tried once again to ban the singing of carols, but this attempt met with the same result as their first. Carols were far too popular and far too much fun to sing. The people simply would not let them go. In fact, the late fifteenth and early sixteenth century saw a "carol revival" in Britain, and people sang carols openly outdoors.

Christmas carols were banned between 1649 and 1660 in England by Oliver Cromwell, who thought Christmas should be a solemn day.

When Protestants fled Europe under pressure from the Catholic Church, they took Christmas carols with them to their new homes across the world. In 1649, John de Brebeur wrote the first American Christmas carol, called "Jesus is Born." In the 1700s, the music of Mendelssohn and Handel was adapted for use as Christmas carols.

Before public carol singing became popular, there were sometimes official carol singers called "waits." They were so named for singing only on Christmas Eve, which was sometimes known as "watchnight" or "waitnight" because the shepherds were watching their sheep when the angels appeared to them. New carol services were created and became popular, as did the custom of singing carols in the streets. The eighteenth century saw a change in the church, and slowly some carols were accepted as part of Christian tradition and permitted back into the church.

Today almost all carols are sung in church, and new carols appear each year. Few maintain a traditional approach to Christmas. One recent carol is all about a teenage mother, and another makes reference to space travel.

FOR FUN

Top 8 Christmas Albums of All Time

8. THE COMPLETE NUTCRACKER SUITE

Although it has been recorded by dozens of different orchestras, the 1988 version by the Kirov Orchestra is one of the best—after all, they're the company for whom Tchaikovsky composed this storybook suite in the first place.

7. WHITE CHRISTMAS

Bing Crosby would have never had to record another song, and he would have still been in the crooner's hall of fame. You will be pleasantly surprised to find many other gems on this classic, including "Jingle Bells" with the Andrews Sisters, and the traditional hymn, "Faith of our Fathers." Bing ends this merry Christmas romp with tributes to the holiday celebrations in Ireland and Hawaii. An all-time must-have.

6. A CHRISTMAS FESTIVAL

With Arthur Fiedler and The Boston Pops. Both lively and thoughtful, this family delight brings you an inspiring blend of secular and religious Christmas music. Among the best of the traditional collections.

5. THE BELLS OF DUBLIN

The Chieftains are joined by the likes of Elvis Costello, Rickie Lee Jones, and Jackson Browne to sing some traditional — and not so traditional — Irish Christmas hymns and songs. Wonderful from beginning to end.

4. CHRISTMAS EVE AND OTHER STORIES

When this album debuted in 1996, fans of rock music paused to hear their favorite carols— on steroids. Trans-Siberian Orchestra's unique combination of electric guitars and synthesizers with a small orchestra provides a high-energy treat, especially the instrumental "Christmas Eve/Sarajevo 12/24."

3. THE CHRISTMAS SONG

Nat King Cole's rich, velvety voice is the only one that should ever be allowed to chronicle chestnuts roasting on an open fire. This is the original and best version of the song that, apart from Christmas carols, defines Christmas music.

2. MANNHEIM STEAMROLLER: CHRISTMAS EXTRAORDINAIRE

The best of several strong Christmas entries from Mannheim Steamroller: Christmas Extraordinaire offers refreshingly innovative interpretations of favorites including "White Christmas," "Away in a Manger," and "Do You Hear What I Hear?" A special treat is the joining of Mannheim's orchestration with Johnny Mathis's honey-sweet vocals for "O Tannenbaum."

1. HIGHLIGHTS FROM HANDEL'S MESSIAH

Heritage Society has gently condensed Handel's inspired oratorio for this "very best of" album, and the Winchester Cathedral Choir and the London Handel Orchestra do the composer proud. Includes the favorites "Worthy Is the Lamb," "Glory to God," "The Hallelujah Chorus," and Handel's soul-stirring conclusion appropriately titled "Amen."

A CHRISTMAS CAROL

Sung to the King in the Presence at White-Hall

R O B E R T   H E R R I C K

MUSIC BY MASTER HENRY LAWES

[CHORUS] What sweeter music can we bring,
Than a carol, for to sing
The birth of this our heavenly King?
Awake the voice! Awake the string!
Heart, ear, and eye, and everything.
Awake! the while the active finger
Runs divisions with the singer.

[VOICE 1] Dark and dulll night, fly hence away,
And give the honor to this day,
That sees December turned to May.

[2] If we may ask the reason, say
The why, and wherefore, all things here
Seem like the springtime of the year?

[3] Why does the chilling winter's morn
Smile like a field beset with corn?
Or smell, like to a mead new-shorn,
Thus on the sudden?

[4] Come and see
The cause why things thus fragrant be:
'Tis He is born, whose quickening birth
Gives life and luster public mirth
To heaven and the under-earth.

[CHORUS] We see Him come, and know Him ours,
Who with his sunshine and his showers
Turns all the patient ground to flowers.

[1] The Darling of the world is come,
And fit it is we find a room
To welcome Him. [2] The nobler part
Of all the house here, is the heart,

[CHORUS] Which we will give him; and bequeath
This holly, and this ivy wreath,
To do him honor; who's our King,
And Lord of all this reveling.

TRIVIA

During the ancient twelve-day Christmas celebration, the log turned was called the "Yule log." Sometimes a piece of the Yule log would be kept to kindle the fire the following winter, to ensure that the good luck carried on from year to year.

FOR FUN

A DOG'S RULES FOR CHRISTMAS

1. Be especially patient with your humans during this time. They may appear to be more stressed out than usual, and they will appreciate long comforting dog leans.

2. They may come home with large bags of things they call gifts. Do not assume that all the gifts are yours.

3. Be tolerant if your humans put decorations on you. They seem to get some special kind of pleasure out of seeing how you look with fake antlers.

4. They may bring a large tree into the house, set it up in a prominent place, and cover it with lights and decorations. Bizarre as this may seem to you, it is an important ritual for your humans, so there are some things you need to know:
   a. Don't pee on the tree.
   b. Don't drink water in the container that holds the tree.
   c. Mind your tail when you are near the tree.
   d. If there are packages under the tree, even ones that smell interesting or that have your name on them, don't rip them open.
   e. Don't chew on the cord that runs from the funny-looking hole in the wall to the tree.

5. Your humans may occasionally invite lots of strangers to come visit during this season. These parties can be lots of fun, but they also call for some discretion on your part:

    a. Not all strangers appreciate kisses and leans,

    b. Don't eat off the buffet table,

    c. Beg for goodies subtly.

    d. Be pleasant, even if unknowing strangers sit on your sofa.

    e. Don't drink out of glasses that are left within your reach.

6. Likewise, your humans may take you visiting. Here your manners will also be important:

    a. Observe all the rules in #4 for trees that may be in other people's houses (4a is particularly important).

    b. Respect the territory of other animals that may live in the house.

    c. Tolerate children.

    d. Turn on your charm big time.

7. A big man with a white beard and a very loud laugh may emerge from your fireplace in the middle of the night.

    Don't Bite him!

A PRAYER BEFORE OPENING PRESENTS

Lord and Giver of all good things, the Magi traveled for miles to bring the Christ child the first Christmas presents. So may we, too, remember with thankful hearts the love that comes with each present we open. We also thank you for the love you have for each of us, and we thank you for the many gifts that you give us, especially the gift of life itself.

Amen.

TRIVIA

If traveling in France during the Christmas season, it is interesting to note that different dishes and dining traditions reign in popularity in different parts of the country. In south France, for instance, a Christmas loaf (pain calendeau) is cut crosswise and is eaten only after the first part has keen given to a poor person. In Brittany, buckwheat cakes with sour cream is the most popular main disk. In Alsace, a roasted goose is the preferred entree. In Burgundy, turkey and chestnuts are favored. In the Paris region, oysters are the favorite holiday disk, followed by a cake shaped like a Yule log.

CHRISTMAS CRAFTS AND HOMEMADE GIFTS

INEXPENSIVE WAYS TO CELEBRATE

Shop Early Online

Shopping online can be done any time of the day or night. You don't have to wait for Thanksgiving to begin your holiday shopping. Put your list together and surf the web to find the best buys. Comparison shop without leaving your home. Take advantage of online stores that offer free shipping.

Consider a Non-Traditional Tree

A Christmas tree can be a huge expense on the Christmas budget. Consider a large new house plant. Another option is an artificial tree that can be used for several years. If you can, purchase your artificial tree after the holidays when retailers mark them down 75 percent.

Stick to the List

It can be tempting to pick up a "great find" while shopping for Christmas gifts. Your list keeps you focused on what you've already determined to purchase.

FOR FUN

A four-year-old boy was asked to return thanks before Christmas dinner. The family members bowed their heads in expectation. He began his prayer, thanking God for all his friends, naming them one by one. Then he thanked God for Mommy, Daddy, brother, sister, Grandma, Grandpa, and all his aunts and uncles. Then he began to thank God for the food.

He gave thanks for the turkey, the dressing, the fruit salad, the cranberry sauce, the pies, the cakes, even the Cool Whip. Then he paused, and everyone waited . . . and waited. After a long silence, the young fellow looked up at his mother and asked, "If I thank God for the broccoli, won't he know that I'm lying?

FACTOIDS

Child singer Jimmy Boyd was twelve years and eleven months old when he sang the Christmas favorite, "I Saw Mommy Kissing Santa Claus." The song hit the top of the pop charts in 1952.

Christmas Around the World

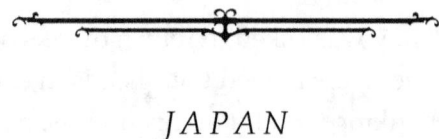

JAPAN

Only 1 percent of Japanese people believe in Christ. Even so, most Japanese people decorate their stores and homes with evergreens during Christmas. They enjoy giving each other gifts. A Buddhist monk they call Hotei-osho is their Santa Claus. He brings presents to each house for the children. Some think he has eyes in the back of his head, so children try to behave like he is nearby.

Among the Christian Japanese, Christmas is not a day for the family — rather they spend it doing nice things for others, especially those who are sick in hospitals. Christmas for those in Sunday schools is the happiest day of the year. On Christmas Eve or Christmas night, the children put on programs that can last for hours. They sing, recite, and put on a drama of the day Jesus was born in Bethlehem.

CHRISTMAS

GEORGE HERBERT

After all pleasures as I rid one day,
My horse and I, both tired, body and mind,
With full cry of affections, quite astray;
I took up the next inn I could find.

There when I came, whom found I but my dear,
My dearest Lord, expecting till the grief
Of pleasures brought me to Him, ready there
To be all passengers' most sweet relief?

Oh Thou, whose glorious, yet contracted light,
Wrapt in night's mantle, stole into a manger;
Since my dark soul and brutish is Thy right,
To man of all beasts be not Thou a stranger:

Furnish and deck my soul, that Thou mayst have
A better lodging, than a rack, or grave.

HANDEL'S MESSIAH

No musical work is more closely associated with the Christmas season than *Messiah* by George Frederick Handel (1685-1759). Handel, however, wrote the work for Easter, not Christmas. The composer was German by birth but became a naturalized Englishman in 1726. He wrote *Messiah* in the summer of 1741, and his first performance was the following spring. Its premiere, in Dublin, was a benefit for prisoners in jail for debt as well as for a hospital and an infirmary. Incidentally, enough money was raised to free 142 unfortunate debtors.

FACTOIDS

In an effort to solicit cash to pay for a charity Christmas dinner in 1891, a large crab pot was set down on a San Francisco street, becoming the first Salvation Army collection kettle.

Bless us Lord, this Christmas,
With quietness of mind;
Teach us to be patient and always be kind.

HELEN STEINER RICE

TRIVIA

The modern Christmas custom of displaying a
wreath on the front door of one's house is
borrowed from ancient Rome's New Year's
celebrations. Romans wished each other "good
health" by exchanging branches of evergreens.
They called these gifts strenae after Strenia, the
goddess of health. It became the custom to bend
these branches into a ring and display them on
doorways.

FOOD TRADITIONS

SCANDINAVIA

In the Nordic countries, Christmas Eve is always celebrated at home. For those who do not have a family, the town halls organize a celebration with a Christmas meal and entertainment. It is very unusual to celebrate Christmas Eve at a restaurant or pub.

A Christmas dinner in a Nordic home is abundant and generous. A typical family will spend the whole day baking and cooking the Christmas meals. The most popular foods are salmon and pickled herring, ham and sausages, salads and rice pudding. Typical drinks are Christmas beer, specially brewed for the celebrations, and liquors.

Swedish Rice Pudding

INGREDIENTS:

4 eggs
1 cup sugar
1/2 teaspoon nutmeg
1 cup cooked rice (do not use minute rice)
1 can Carnation evaporated milk (12 fluid ounces)
1/2-1/4 cup low-fat milk
2-3 tablespoons butter, softened
cinnamon

DIRECTIONS:

In a medium-sized bowl, beat eggs lightly, add sugar, and beat a little more. Add nutmeg. Add cooked rice to the mixture. Add Carnation evaporated milk and stir.

Pour into a 2-quart dish and add low-fat milk. Sprinkle cinnamon on top. Add butter (about 1/2 tablespoon at a time).

Bake in a 325° F oven for 1.5 hours or until the pudding's top moves a little in the center if you push it gently.

Makes approximately 6 servings.

CHRISTMAS CRAFTS AND HOMEMADE GIFTS

INEXPENSIVE WAYS TO CELEBRATE

Make the Kids a Part of the Team

Learning to give the gift of themselves can be the most valuable memory your children discover this holiday season!

Buy white or red place mats and let your children create their own artwork with fabric crayons. A place mat can be made for each guest for Christmas dinner. Your children will feel an important part of the festivities.

Make paper angels and have your children write short messages to each family member stating the things about that person for which they are thankful. Your children will have an opportunity to think beyond the commercialism of the day to appreciate the blessings they already have.

Allow your children to make this year's Christmas cards. Simply buy blank cards at your favorite office supply store and let your children loose with magic markers. They can even compose a poem and message for each recipient.

Have your children come up with small tasks they can easily do—like taking out the trash. They can then write those tasks on plain paper angels they make themselves. Have them deliver the angels to elderly neighbors as a gift of sharing for the holiday season.

A CHILDREN'S PRAYER

O holy Child of Bethlehem,
Descend to us, we pray;
Cast out our sin and enter in.
Be born in us to-day.
Amen.

I HEARD THE BELLS ON CHRISTMAS DAY

One of America's best-known poets, Henry Wadsworth Longfellow (1807-1882), contributed to the wealth of carols sung each Christmas season, when he composed the words to "I Heard the Bells on Christmas Day" on December 25, 1864. The carol was originally a poem containing seven stanzas. When Longfellow penned the words to his poem, America was still months away from Lee's surrender to Grant at Appomattox Court House on April 9, 1865. His poem reflected the prior years of the war's despair, while ending with a confident hope of triumphant peace.

Because two stanzas contained references to the Civil War, they were omitted, and the remaining five stanzas were slightly rearranged in 1872 by John Baptiste Calkin (1827-1905), who also gave us the lovely tune.

FACTOIDS
The puritans forbade the singing
of Christmas carols.

Christmas Around the World

GERMANY

After the Reformation, German Christians created a character called *das Christkindl*, or *das Christkind*. Though similar to the Baby Jesus, it evolved into an adult angel, often a woman dressed in white fur who distributed toys carried by a reindeer.

Over the years, *der Weinachtsmann*, or German Santa Claus, displaced the celebration of the *Christkindl*. Because Germany has many regions each with its own customs, Germany has several versions of Santa Claus, including Saint Nicholas, *Reprecht, Pelnickel*, and *Aschenmann*.

On the eve of December 6, Saint Nicholas is said to make his rounds carrying a list of all the children. According to legend, he leaves gifts for the good little kids and coal for the naughty ones. German children decorate their Christmas lists with pictures and then leave them on windowsills overnight, weighed down with a little sugar so they won't be missed by Saint Nicholas.

The Christmas tree, or *Tannenbaum*, is a mainstay in German Christmas decorations. It has changed somewhat through history, shedding its dangerous open-flame candles in favor of safer electric lights. Gingerbread figures are also a great tradition from Germany.

In Germany, Christmas is usually celebrated on Christmas Eve.

CHRISTMAS BELLS

HENRY WADSWORTH LONGFELLOW

I heard the bells on Christmas Day
Their old, familiar carols play,
And wild and sweet
The words repeat
Of peace on earth, good-will to men!

And thought how, as the day had come,
The belfries of all Christendom
Had rolled along
The unbroken song
Of peace on earth, good-will to men!

Till, ringing, singing on its way
The world revolved from night to day,
A voice, a chime,
A chant sublime
Of peace on earth, good-will to men!

Then from each black, accursed mouth
The cannon thundered in the South,
And with the sound
The carols drowned
Of peace on earth, good-will to men!

And in despair I bowed my head;
"There is no peace on earth," I said;
"For hate is strong,
And mocks the song
Of peace on earth, good-will to men!"

Then pealed the tells more loud and deep
"God is not dead; nor doth he sleep!
The Wrong skall fail,
The Right prevail;
With peace on earth, good-will to men!"

So remember while December
Brings the only Christmas day,
In the year let there be Christmas
In the things you do and say.
ANONYMOUS

201

Traditions

THE STORY OF THE POINSETTIA

Poinsettias are a beautiful and extremely popular Christmas decoration, used worldwide in great abundance, both commercially and in religious settings. This lush, beautiful flower has a heartwarming legend which involves a Christmas miracle for a little Mexican peasant girl by the name of Maria.

The legend tells that Maria lived on a poor family farm in a small village in Mexico. This village took great delight in offering gifts to the Baby Jesus at Christmas time, and offerings were made in glorious decorations in and around the church. The village children would participate by making gifts to offer the Baby Jesus on Christmas Eve.

Even though she was very poor, Maria wanted to make a special offering to Jesus. She wanted so badly to march with the other children in the procession at the church, but it was Christmas Eve and she had nothing.

Suddenly she heard a voice speaking to her, "Child, Jesus will love anything that you bring to him from your heart. It's your love for him that makes your gift special." She looked around, but she saw no one. She looked up and saw a brilliant star. Could that star be speaking to her?

Anything you bring, the voice had said. Maria spied some tall green weeds nearby and filled her arms with them and wrapped them in her manto. She ran to the church. By the time she got there everyone was inside the church.

Suddenly Maria was embarrassed. She was dressed poorly, and her gift, while it came from her heart, was just an armload of weeds. The village priest spotted Maria near the back of the church.

"Maria, Maria! Where is your gift? Hurry! Come quickly!"

The Padre saw how embarrassed and frightened she was, and he spoke tenderly to her. "Maria, come up here and see the Baby Jesus. There's room for one more gift."

Maria began to walk carefully down the aisle toward the Baby, The people around her began to ask each other what her gift could be. What did she carry under her manto? Maria said a prayer, and then she closed her eyes and opened her manto and let the weeds tumble out.

"Look! Look at those glorious flowers!" the villagers gasped.

Startled. Maria opened her eyes. She gasped! Each weed now had a flaming bright scarlet star! Maria's love for Jesus had created a miracle, and from that day to this, every poinsettia carries the deep red coloring that was born that night in a little girl's heart.

While some stories claim that Maria laid the miracle flowers at the feet of the Baby Jesus, some claim that they were offered to the Virgin Mary. Either way, there is actually a grain of truth in the story. The poinsettia does originate from Central America. And even though the legend is touching, the truth is just as interesting.

Joel Robert Poinsett, for whom the poinsettia was named, was born in Charleston in 1759. He became a planter, botanist, and statesman. He was also our country's first minister to Mexico, where he found the plant and brought it back to Charleston in 1829.

The bright, blood-red poinsettia has become the most popular of all Christmas flowers and is used throughout the world during the Christmas season. The star of the leaf is said to represent the star that stood over the Christ Child. The red Bower stands for the blood of the male infants that King Herod had slain. The red flower also represents the shed blood of Christ who came to be our Savior. Its bright, star-like flower is a natural reminder of the Star of Bethlehem.

There are many versions of the Christmas miracle of the weeds turning into scarlet flowers. But because it is believed that the miracle did happen, they are called Flores de Noche Buena, or Flowers of the Holy Night—and they have continued to bloom during Christmas ever since.

CHRISTMAS

GEORGE HERBERT

The shepherds sing; and shall I silent be?
My God, no hymn for Thee?
My soul is a shepherd too; a flock it feeds
Of thoughts, and words, and deeds.
The pasture is Thy word: the streams, Thy grace
Enriching all the place.
Shepherd and flock shall sing, and all my powers
Out-sing the daylight hours.
Then will we chide the sun for letting night
Take up his place and right:
We sing one common Lord; wherefore he should
Himself the candle hold.
I will go searching, till I find a sun
Shall stay, till we have done;
A willing shiner, that shall shine as gladly,
As frost-nipped suns look sadly.
Then will we sing, and shine all our own day,
And one another pay:
His beams shall cheer my breast, and both so twine,
Till ev'n His beams sing, and my music shine.

WE THREE KINGS

The traditional belief that the Magi were kings dates from the sixth century. The church taught that Jesus was the King of Kings, and, to reinforce their point, church leaders felt it necessary to show that he had been treated as royalty. The Magi were thus converted into kings because a royal child should be visited by royalty to demonstrate his importance.

Most experts are convinced that the Magi were priests and/or astrologers. Certainly, the Magi were watchers of the sky and astrologers (the difference between astrology and astronomy was not to be defined for many centuries) and would have understood the meaning of the Star in terms of their knowledge.

FACTOIDS
In Britain, the Holy Days and Fasting Days
Act of 1551, which has not yet been repealed,
states that every citizen must attend a
Christian church service on Christmas Day, ad
must not use any kind of vehicle to get to the
service.

WE THREE KINGS

JOHN H. HOPKINS JR.

We three kings of Orient are:
Bearing gifts, we traverse afar.
Field and fountain, moor and mountain,
Following yonder star.

O Star of Wonder, Star of Night,
Star with Royal Beauty bright,
Westward leading, still proceeding,
Guide us to Thy perfect Light.

Born a king on Bethlehem's plain,
Gold I bring to crown Him again,
King forever, ceasing never
Over us all to reign.

O Star of Wonder, Star of Night,
Star with Royal Beauty bright,
Westward leading, still proceeding,
Guide us to Thy perfect Light.

Frankincense to offer have I;
Incense owns a Deity nigh:
Prayer and praising, all men raising,
Worship Him, God on high.

O Star of Wonder, Star of Night,
Star with Royal Beauty bright,
Westward leading, still proceeding,
Guide us to Thy perfect Light.

Myrrh is mine; its bitter perfume;
Breathes a life of gathering gloom —
Sorr'wing, sighing, bleeding, dying,
Sealed in stone-cold tomb.

O Star of Wonder, Star of Night,
Star with Royal Beauty bright,
Westward leading, still proceeding,
Guide us to Thy perfect Light.

Glorious now behold Him arise,
King and God and sacrifice;
Heav'n sings Halleluia;
Hallelujah the earth replies.

O Star of Wonder, Star of Night,
Star with Royal Beauty bright,
Westward leading, still proceeding,
Guide us to Thy perfect Light.

FOR FUN

HOW TO SAY "MERRY CHRISTMAS" AROUND THE WORLD

Arabic: Milad Majid

Bengali: Shuvo Naba Barsha

Brazilian: Boas Festas

Bulgarian: Tchestita Koleda

Chinese (Mandarin): Kung His Hsin Nien bing Chu Shen Tan

(Catonese): Gun Tso Sun Tan'Gung Haw Sun

Danish: Glaedelig Jul

Dutch: Vrolijk Kerstfeest or Zalig Kerstfeast!

Eskimo (inupik): Jutdlime pivdluarit ukiortame pivdluaritlo!

Finnish: Hyvaa joulua

French: Joyeux Noel

German: Fröehliche Weihnachten

Greek: Kala Christouyenna!

Hawaiian: Mele Kalikimaka

Hebrew: Mo'adim Lesimkha

Hindi: Shub Naya Baras

Hungarian: Kellemes Karacsonyi unnepeket
Iraqi: Idah Saidan Wa Sanah Jadidah
Italian: Buone Feste Natalizie
Japanese: Shinnen omedeto
Korean: Sung Tan Chuk Ha
Navajo: Merry Keshmish
Norwegian: God Jul, or Gledelig Jul
Philippines: Maligayan Pasko!
Polish: Wesolych Swiat Bozego Narodzenia or Boze
Narodzenie
Portuguese: Feliz Natal
Russian: Pozdrevlyayu s prazdnikom Rozhdestva is
Novim Godom
Spanish: Feliz Navidad
Swedish: God Jul
Turkish: Noeliniz Ve Yeni Yiliniz Kutlu Olsun
Vietnamese: Chung Mung Giang Sinh

FACTOIDS
*The first printed reference to Christmas trees
appeared in Germany in 1531.*

TRIVIA

FAMOUS – AND INFAMOUS – PEOPLE BORN ON CHRISTMAS DAY

1642: Sir Isaac Newton (mathematician)

1821: Clara Barton (nurse, founder of the American Red Cross)

1887: Conrad Hilton (hotel magnate)

1899: Humphrey Bogart (Academy Award – winning actor: *The African Queen* [1951])

1907: Cat (Cabell) Calloway (bandleader, singer: "Minnie the Moocher")

1918: Anwar el-Sadat (Egyptian president, Nobel Peace Prize winner with Israel's Menachim Begin [1978])

1924: Rod Sterling (actor: *The Twilight Zone*)

1932: Little Richard (Penniman) (singer: "Good Golly Miss Molly")

1937: O'Kelly Isley (Grammy Award – winning group, The Isley Brothers: "It's Your Thing" [1969])

1946: Jimmy Buffett (songwriter, singer: "Margaritaville")

1948: Barbara Mandrell (CMA Entertainer of the Year [1980, 1981])

1949: Sissy (Mary) Spacek (Academy Award-winning actress: *Coal Miner's Daughter* [1980])

Christmas Around the World

POLAND

Advent is an important season in the Polish year, with special church services known as *Roraty* held every morning at six. The four Sundays of Advent are said to represent the 4,000 years of waiting for Christ. During Advent and in some homes on Christmas Eve, beeswax is poured on water and fortunes are told from the shapes that emerge.

Beautifully lit Christmas trees are placed in all public arenas and are traditionally decorated with shiny apples, beautifully wrapped chocolate, and homemade decorations and candles. In many homes, sparklers are hung on the tree branches. Sometimes the trees are left standing until February 2, the feast day of Saint Mary of the Candle of Lightning.

Traditionally Christmas Eve is a time for young women to think of marriage and to look for signs as to whether or not they will be manned in the coming year. For farmers it is the time to look for signs of what the next year will bring in terms of weather. On Christmas Eve, tradition states that a man should be the first person to cross the threshold into a house.

A traditional Polish food at Christmas is *oplatek*, a piece of bread pressed with a holy picture on the surface. People once carried *oplatek* from house to house to wish their neighbors a Merry Christmas. Nowadays, the bread is mostly shared with family members and immediate neighbors. As each person shares the bread, he or she has to do two things: forgive any hurts that have occurred over the past year, and wish the person all the happiness in the coming year.

A TRADITIONAL IRISH CHRISTMAS

The light of the Christmas star to you
The warmth of home and hearth to you
The cheer and goodwill of friends to you
The hope of a childlike heart to you
The joy of a thousand angels to you
The love of the Son and God's peace to you.

Every time we love, every time we give,
it's Christmas.
DALE EVANS ROGERS

A PRAYER FOR CHRISTMAS MORNING

The day of joy returns, Father in heaven, and crowns another year with peace and goodwill. Help us rightly to remember the birth of Jesus, that we may share in the song of the angels, the gladness of the shepherds, and the worship of the wise men.

Close the doors of hate and open the doors of love all over the world . . .

Let kindness come with every gift and good desires with every greeting. Deliver us from evil, by the blessing that Christ brings, and teach us to be merry with clean hearts.

May the Christmas morning make us happy to be thy children, and the Christmas evening bring us to our bed with grateful thoughts, forgiving and forgiven, for Jesus' sake.

Amen.

THE SHEPHERDS

HENRY VAUGHAN

Sweet, harmless lives! (on whose holy leisure
Waits innocence and pleasure),
Whose leaders to those pastures, and clear springs,
Were patriarchs, saints, and kings,
How happened it that in the dead of night
You only saw true light,
While Palestine was fast asleep, and lay
Without one thought of day?
Was it because those first and blessed swains
Were pilgrims on those plains
When they received the promise, for which now
'Twas there first shown to you?
'Tis true, He loves that dust whereon they go
That serve Him here below,
And therefore might for memory of those
His love there first disclose;
But wretched Salem, once His love, must now
No voice, nor vision know,
Her stately piles with all their height and pride
Now languished and died,
And Bethlem's humble cotes above them stepped
While all her seers slept;
Her cedar, fir, hewed stones and gold were all
Polluted through their fall,
And those once sacred mansions were now
Mere emptiness and show;

This made the angel call at reeds and thatch,
Yet where the shepherds watch,
And God's own lodging (though He could not lack)
To be a common rack;
No costly pride, no soft-clothed luxury
In those thin cells could lie,
Each stirring wind and storm blew through their cots
Which never harbored plots,
Only content, and love, and humble joys
Lived there without all noise,
Perhaps some harmless cares for the next day
Did in their bosoms play,
As where to lead their sheep, what silent nook,
What springs or shades to look,
But that was all; and now with gladsome care
They for the town prepare,
They leave their flock, and in a busy talk
All towards Bethlem walk
To see their souls' Great Shepherd, Who was come
To bring all stragglers home,
Where now they find Him out, and taught before
That Lamb of God adore,
That Lamb whose days great kings and prophets wished
And longed to see, but missed.
The first light they beheld was bright and gay
And turned their night to day,
But to this later light they saw in Him,
Their day was dark, and dim.

THERE'S A SONG IN THE AIR

"There's a Song in the Air" was written by Josiah Gilbert Holland, a one-time high-school dropout because of poor health, who tried his hand successively at photography and calligraphy before enrolling in a medical school. After earning his medical degree and practicing his profession for a few years, he gave up medicine to become the owner and editor of a newspaper. He remained a writer, poet, novelist, and editor until his death. The four stanzas of "There's a Song in the Air" appeared in print for the first time in 1872 in a book of his poems.

Holland's Christmas poem became very popular, and when a new hymnal was being prepared for publication in 1905, three noted composers submitted melodies for "There's a Song in the Air." Since the publishers considered all three tunes to be excellent, the three were printed in the new hymnal, but the melody composed by Karl Harrington became the most preferred and memorable.

Professor Karl Harrington, a university Latin teacher and part-time musician, came from a very musical and creative family. His father had been one of the musical editors of a hymnal, and quite early in life Karl had tried his hand at composing hymn tunes on the small organ that stood in the living room of the Harrington home. Many years later, his father bought a new and larger parlor organ. When the new instrument was delivered, he gave the smaller organ to Karl, who promptly moved it to his vacation retreat. While spending some time there in July 1904, on a sudden impulse, he sat at the old organ and proceeded to compose his sweeping, melodic tune for Holland's poem.

FOOD TRADITIONS

SCANDINAVIA

Swedish Dill Salmon (Gravlax)

Note: This recipe requires advance preparation.

INGREDIENTS:

4 pounds fresh salmon, center cut
3.5 tablespoons coarse salt
3.5 tablespoons sugar
4 teaspoons white peppercorns, crushed
1 bunch fresh dill

GRAVLAXSAS:

2 tablespoons mild mustard
1 teaspoon mustard powder
1 tablespoon sugar
1.5 tablespoons wine vinegar
3 tablespoons salad oil
3 tablespoons chopped fresh dill
salt and pepper

DIRECTIONS:

SALMON:

Remove the backbone and other bones from the salmon and cut in half lengthwise. Combine the salt, sugar, and pepper, and rub over the insides of the fish. Place one piece, skin side down, in a large bowl or serving dish. Place the dill over the salmon. Top with the other piece of fish, skin side up. Place a heavy platter over the salmon and weight it down.

Refrigerate, covered, for 24 hours. Turn the fish once or twice during this time. When finished, remove the salmon from the dish and scrape off the seasonings and dill. Cut off skin and slice the salmon diagonally into thin slices.

GRAVLAXSAS:

Combine the mustard, sugar, and vinegar in a bowl and mix well together to make a paste. Slowly add the oil, beating well after each addition. Beat until the sauce is the consistency of mayonnaise. Season with salt and pepper and add the dill.

Makes a half cup.

Serve the slices of salmon garnished with fresh dill and slices or pieces of salmon skin with gravlaxsas. Makes 8 to 10 servings.

THERE'S A SONG IN THE AIR

JOSIAH G. HOLLAND

There's a song in the air!
There's a star in the sky!
There's a mother's deep prayer,
And a baby's low cry!
And the star rains its fire while the beautiful sing,
For the manger of Bethlehem cradles a King!

There's a tumult of joy
O'er the wonderful birth,
For the virgin's sweet boy
Is the Lord of the earth.
Ay! The star rains its fire while the beautiful sing,
For the manger of Bethlehem cradles a King!

In the light of that star
Lie the ages impearled;
And that song from afar
Has swept over the world.
Ev'ry hearth is aflame, and the beautiful sing
In the homes of the nations that Jesus is King!

We rejoice in the light,
And we echo the song
That comes down thru the night
From the heavenly throng.
Ay! We shout to the lovely evangel they bring,
And we greet in his cradle our Savior and King!

VOICES IN THE MIST

ALFRED, LORD TENNYSON

The time draws near the birth of Christ:
The moon is hid; the night is still;
The Christmas bells from hill to hill
Answer each other in the mist.

Four voices of four hamlets round,
From far and near, on mead and moor,
Swell out and fail, as if a door
Were shut between me and the sound:

Each voice four changes on the wind,
That now dilate, and now decrease,
Peace and goodwill, goodwill and peace,
Peace and goodwill, to all mankind.

FACTOIDS
Formally called Kiritimati, Christmas Island in the
Indian Ocean is 52 square miles.

TRIVIA

Christmas trees are known to have been popular in Germany as far back as the sixteenth century. In England, they became popular after Queen Victoria's husband, Albert, who came from Germany, made the decorating of a tree part of the celebrations at Windsor Castle.

FOR FUN

TOP 10 WORST GIFTS TO GIVE YOUR WIFE

10. Buns of Steel
9. The Clapper
8. A set of Ginsu knives
7. Cooking for Dummies
6. A taxidermy of Spot, the recently deceased family dog
5. Wrestlemania 1-12
4. A kitchen appliance
3. A grooming appliance
2. Anything practical
1. Anything named "Chia"

SHEPHERDS UP!

On Christmas morning in Austria, the father of the family awakens and sings this traditional carol — sung only once a year — to wake the other members of the family. The family gathers and sings verse after verse — each verse a step higher — until everyone is awake.

Shepherds, up, your watch to take!
Your time of sleep is ending,
For the Good Shepherd is awake,
His earthly flock attending.
Haste to the manger, to Mary, so mild,
Come and adore him, the heavenly Child.

FOOD TRADITIONS

LEBANON

Baklava (Middle Eastern Nut-Filled Multilayered Pastry)

The recipes below were taken from
The World of Jewish Desserts by Gil Marks.

INGREDIENTS:

SYRUP:

3 cups sugar, or 2 cups sugar and 1 cup honey
1.5 cups water
2 tablespoons lemon juice
2 tablespoons light corn syrup (optional)
2 (3-inch) sticks cinnamon (optional)
4 to 6 whole cloves, or 1/2 teaspoon ground cardamom (optional)

FILLING:

1 pound blanched almonds, pistachios, walnuts, or any
combination, finely chopped or coarsely ground (about 4 cups)
1/4 cup sugar
1 to 2 teaspoons ground cinnamon
1/4 teaspoon ground cloves or cardamom (optional)
1 pound (about 24 sheets) phyllo dough
1 cup (2 sticks) melted butter or vegetable oil

DIRECTIONS:

To make the syrup: stir the sugar, water, lemon juice, and if using, the corn syrup, cinnamon sticks, and/or cloves over low heat until the sugar dissolves, about 5 minutes. Stop stirring, increase the heat to medium, and cook until the mixture is slightly syrupy, about 3 minutes (it will register 225° F on a candy thermometer). Discard the cinnamon sticks and whole cloves. Let cool.

To make the filling: combine all the filling ingredients.

Preheat the oven to 350° F. Grease a 12 x 9-inch or 13 x 9- inch baking pan or 15 x 10-inch jelly roll pan.

Place a sheet of phyllo in the prepared pan and lightly brush with butter. Repeat with 7 more sheets, brushing each sheet lightly with butter. Spread with half of the filling.

Top with 8 more sheets, brushing each sheet with butter. Use any torn sheets in the middle layer. Spread with the remaining nut mixture and end with a top layer of 8 sheets, continuing to brush each with butter. Trim any overhanging edges.

Using a sharp knife, cut 6 equal lengthwise strips (about 1.75 inches wide) through the top layer of pastry. Make 1.5 inch-wide diagonal cuts across the strips to form diamond shapes.

Just before baking, lightly sprinkle the top of the pastry with cold water. This inhibits the pastry from curling. Bake for 20 minutes. Reduce the heat to 300° F. and bake until golden brown, about 15 additional minutes.

Cut through the scored lines. Drizzle the cooled syrup slowly over the hot baklava and let cool for at least 4 hours. Cover and store at room temperature for up to 1 week. If the baklava dries out while being stored, drizzle with a little additional hot syrup.

VARIATIONS:

Instead of brushing each layer of phyllo with butter, cut the unbaked baklava into diamonds all the way through, drizzle with 1 cup vegetable oil, and let stand for 10 minutes before baking.

PERSIAN BAKLAVA:

Using the almonds and cardamom in the filling: Omit the lemon juice and cinnamon from the syrup and add 1/4 cup rose water or 1 tablespoon orange blossom water after it has cooled.

PAKLAVA (AZERBAIJANI BAKLAVA):

For the filling, use 2 cups blanched almonds, 2 cups unsalted pistachios, 1/4 cup sugar, 1 teaspoon ground cardamom, and 1 teaspoon ground cinnamon. Crush 1/4 teaspoon saffron threads and let steep in 3 tablespoons of the melted butter for 15 minutes and use to brush the top sheet of phyllo.

A PRAYER WHILE WRAPPING GIFTS

Dear Lord, I am tired. I sit here surrounded by ribbons and paper, gifts and tags, and I struggle to feel the spirit of giving. I can barely remember which gift is for whom, and at moments it all seems so far from your birth. Help me to take this moment to think of the many gifts you have given to me, the many ways your grace has blessed my life. Help me to remember that each gift is a tiny mirror of the generosity I see so clearly in your life and of the many ways you shower me with such lavish and undeserved love. Let me sit here for just a moment and feel that joy in my heart. Thank you. Thank you.

CHRISTMAS CAROL

HENRY WADSWORTH LONGFELLOW

When Christ was born in Bethlehem,
'Twas night, but seemed the noon of day;
The stars, whose light
Was pure and bright,
Shone with unwavering ray;
But one, one glorious star
Guided the Eastern Magi from afar.

Then peace was spread throughout the land;
The lion fed beside the tender lamb;
And with the kid,
To pasture led,
The spotted leopard fed;
In peace, the calf and bear,
The wolf and lamb reposed together there.

CHRISTMAS CRAFTS AND HOMEMADE GIFTS

INEXPENSIVE WAYS TO CELEBRATE

Give the Gift of Quality Time

1. Attend a Christmas play or performance, such as *A Christmas Carol*, *The Nutcracker*, or *Messiah*. Even if you are unable to attend a performance, you may be able to watch it at home in front of a cozy fire. Serve homemade popcorn and have fun.

2. Watch some old movies, such as *It's a Wonderful Life* or *The Sound of Music*.

3. Begin a giant jigsaw puzzle on December 1 and try to finish it by New Year's Day.

4. Collect your children's old crayons. Peel and place them into Christmas candy molds. Place in pans of hot water to melt, or if the molds are heat resistant, melt at low setting in the microwave or oven. Cool and let your children create Christmas cards and pictures for others with their "new crayons."

5. Have a birthday party for Jesus. This can be a family activity, or you may want to have a real birthday party with your children's friends.

6. Take time to share yourselves with others. Christmas is a lonely time for shut-ins, widows, and residents at a nursing home. After your children become familiar with the Christmas story, take them to

a retirement center or a shut-in and let them tell the story. Both the teller and the hearers will be blessed!

7. Sponsor an underprivileged child or buy Christmas gifts for children of prisoners (Angel Tree Project). Have your children get involved in selecting the gifts. One of our best Christmases was the year we decided to celebrate simply and buy gifts for a needy family.

8. Begin a Christmas journal. Record your family events. In future years, you can reminisce about past holiday seasons.

9. Put together a Christmas photo scrapbook. Include pictures as well as favorite cards and letters.

JOY TO THE WORLD

"Joy to the World" was written by Isaac Watts (1674-1748), a respected writer but not a handsome man. A young lady who had fallen in love with him from his writings asked him to marry her. When she saw him in person, however, she changed her mind and took back the offer. She wrote later that Isaac Watts was "only five feet tall, with a shallow face, hooked nose, prominent cheek bones, small eyes, and deathlike color . . . I admired the jewel but not the casket [box]."

Though he didn't experience much success with women, he became a prolific writer. Besides "Joy to the World," "When I Survey the Wondrous Cross," "O God, Our Help in Ages Past," "Alas! And Did My Savior Bleed," and "I Sing the Mighty Power of God" are in most hymnals today. In fact, today he is known as the "father of hymnody."

When he was dying, Watts said, "I am just waiting to see what God will do with me; it is good to say, what, when, and where God pleases. The business of a Christian is to do the will of God. If God should raise me up again, and use me to save a soul, that will be worth living for. If he has no more service for me, I can say, through grace, I am ready; I could without alarm if God please, lay back my head on my pillow and die this afternoon or night. My sins are all pardoned through the blood of Christ."

Many years after Watts's death, Dr. Lowell Mason (1792-1872) put the words to "Joy to the World" to music based on *Messiah* by Frederick Handel (1685-1759), a contemporary of Watts. When he tried to publish his first set of musical works, however, it was rejected. Finally, the Handel and Haydn Society of Boston accepted it. Lowell eventually became president over the society that published his works.

"Joy to the World" is now universally sung as one of the most joyous songs of Christmas.

A PRAYER FOR THOSE CELEBRATING CHRISTMAS AFTER THE LOSS OF A LOVED ONE

*God of compassion, there is such a hole in my heart!
Today should be a day of joy, but I feel only the
emptiness and loss of someone so beloved. While the
world celebrates around me, I remember Christmas
celebrations of the past, and I long to have my loved one
with me. I bring my sorrows to you, Lord, like some odd
gift of the Magi and dump them at your feet. In my
blind tears I wonder if anyone can possibly understand
the depth of my sadness.*

*Yes, you can. You sent your Son to be with us in our
deepest sorrows, and I know that even though I might
not feel it at this minute, you are here with me, grieving
with me, caring for me in my sadness, and loving me.
Dearest Lord, help me to turn to the one I miss so much
today and speak. Help me heal the loss of our parting,
and help me not to regret the things I didn't say.
Sorrow tears at my heart, but today I ask that my loss
soften my heart and make me more compassionate with
everyone I meet. Amen.*

CHRISTMAS EVERYWHERE

PHILLIPS BROOKS

EVERYWHERE, everywhere, Christmas tonight!
Christmas in lands of the fir-tree and pine,
Christmas in lands of the palm-tree and vine,
Christmas where snow peaks stand solemn and white,
Christmas where cornfields stand sunny and bright.
Christmas where children are hopeful and gay,
Christmas where old men are patient and gray,
Christmas where peace, like a dove in his flight,
Broods o're brave men in the thick of the fight;
Everywhere, everywhere, Christmas tonight!
For the Christ-child who comes is the Master of all;
No palace too great, no cottage too small.

May peace be your gift at Christmas
and your blessing all year through!
UNKNOWN

Christmas Around the World

NORWAY

Norwegian children always remember the little gnome *fjosnissen* at Christmastime. He guards all the farm animals and plays tricks on the children if they forget to place a bowl of special porridge for him. Norwegians also love to eat this porridge — *lillejulaften* — on December 23. The person who finds the almond hidden inside gets a prize.

In early days, Norway had a gift-bearing goat-like, creature known as *Julebukk*, or Christmas buck. During the early Christian era, the goat began to take the form of the devil. Some Norwegians believed several creatures would fly by their homes on certain nights to ensure that proper Christmas preparations were underway. If they weren't, those responsible would be punished.

The Christmas tree, or *juletre*, is a spruce or pine tree often decorated with candles, apples, comets, straw ornaments, glass balls, and tinsel. Many Norwegians still follow the tradition of the "seven kinds," which requires that seven kinds of cookies or sweet breads be on the table at Christmas. A favorite holiday cookie is called a *sand kager*, which is made by mixing butter, sugar, flour, and chopped almonds and pressing the dough into a tin. The dough is baked until golden brown and cut into squares.

On the dark December afternoons, children go from house to house asking for goodies. Norwegians traditionally eat lye-treated codfish (lutefisk) and wash it down with boiled potatoes, rice porridge, gingerbread, and punch.

Christmas in Norway begins with the Saint Lucia ceremony on December 13. At the crack of dawn, the family's youngest daughter puts on a white robe with a sash and a crown with evergreens and tall, lighted candles. Accompanied by the other children, she wakes her parents and serves them coffee and Lucia buns, or *lussekatter*. On December 24, many people go to a church service before they gather for Christmas Eve dinner. On Christmas Day, people have a big brunch at noon or dinner in the afternoon for friends and family.

FOOD TRADITIONS

LEBANON

About two weeks before Christmas the Lebanese plant seeds such as chickpeas, wheat grains, beans, and lentils in cotton wool. They water the seeds every day, and by Christmas the seeds have shoots about six inches in height. They use the shoots to surround the manger in nativity scenes.

Traditionally people visit friends on Christmas morning and are offered coffee, liqueurs, and sugared almonds. Lunch at Christmas is the most important meal of the season, and the whole family gathers together for it, usually at grandparents' or the eldest son's home. The meal consists of chicken and rice, turkey, roast duck, Lebanese salad (*tabbouleh*), crushed boiled wheat (*bulgur*) mixed with meat, onion, salt and pepper (*kubbeh*), and pastries such as a honey cake (*baklava*) or *Buche de Noel* may be served.

Lebanese Tabbouleh

This recipe was taken from the June 2002 issue of Gourmet magazine.

INGREDIENTS:

1/2 cup fine bulgur wheat
3 tablespoons olive oil
1 cup boiling-hot water
2 cups finely chopped fresh flat-leaf parsley (from 3 bunches)
1/2 cup finely chopped fresh mint
2 medium tomatoes, cut into 1/4-inch pieces
1/2 seedless cucumber*, peeled, cored, and cut into 1/4-inch pieces
3 tablespoons fresh lemon juice
3/4 teaspoon salt
1/4 teaspoon black pepper

DIRECTIONS:

Stir together bulgur and 1 tablespoon oil in a heatproof bowl. Pour boiling water over the mixture, then cover bowl tightly with plastic wrap and let stand 15 minutes. Drain in a sieve, pressing on bulgur to remove any excess liquid.

Transfer bulgur to a bowl and toss with remaining ingredients, including 2 tablespoons oil, until combined well.

*These long, narrow cucumbers are often marketed as "European" and are usually sold in plastic wrap to protect their thin, delicate, unwaxed skin.

FOR FUN

CHRISTMAS MONDEGREENS

The term "mondegreen" — representing a series of words resulting from the mishearing of a statement or song lyric — is generally attributed to Sylvia Wright, who is credited with coining the neologism in a 1954 Harper's column. Ms. Wright was chagrined to discover that for many years she had misunderstood the last line of the first stanza in the Scottish folk ballad "The Bonny Earl of Murray," which reads:

Ye Highlands and ye Lawlands,
Oh! Where ha'e ye been:
They ha'e slain the Earl of Murray,
And they laid him on the Green.

MS. WRIGHT MISHEARD THIS STANZA AS:

Ye Highlands and ye Lawlands,
Oh! Where ha'e ye been:
They ha'e slain the Earl of Murray,
And Lady Mondegreen.

*BELOW ARE SOME MORE EXAMPLES OF
MONDEGREENS:*

*In the meadow we can build a snowman;
Then pretend that he is sparse and brown.*
"WINTER WONDERLAND"

*Everybody knows a turkey, handsome Mr. Soul
Help to make the season bright.*
"THE CHRISTMAS SONG"

Round John Virgin, mother and child . . .
"SILENT NIGHT"

Then one froggy Christmas eve . . .
"RUDOLPH THE RED-NOSED REINDEER"

Deck the Halls with Buddy Holly.
"DECK THE HALLS"

On the first day of Christmas
my tulip gave to me.
"THE TWELVE DAYS OF CHRISTMAS"

He's makin' a list, chicken and rice.
"SANTA CLAUS IS COMIN' TO TOWN"

Noel. Noel, Barney's the king of Israel.
"THE FIRST NOEL"

With the jelly toast proclaim.
"HARK! THE HERALD ANGELS SING"

Olive, the other reindeer.
"RUDOLPH THE RED-NOSED REINDEER"

Oh, what fun it is to ride with one horse,
soap, and sleigh.
"JINGLE BELLS"

You'll tell Carol, "Be a skunk, I require."
"THE CHRISTMAS SONG"

Good Tidings we bring to you and your kid.
"WE WISH YOU A MERRY CHRISTMAS"

I WONDER AS I WANDER

This Appalachian carol was gathered in Murphy, North Carolina, in 1933 by John Jacob Niles (1892-1980), a leading American folk-song collector, who, it is said, paid young traveling Annie Morgan twenty-five cents an hour to sing it until he had memorized it.

I wonder as I wander out under the sky,
How Jesus the Savior did come for to die
For poor on'ry people like you and like I . . .
I wonder as I wander out under the sky.

When Mary birthed Jesus, twas in a cow's stall,
With wise men and farmers and shepherds and all.
But high from God's heaven a star's light did fall,
And the promise of ages it then did recall.

If Jesus had wanted for any wee tiling,
A star in the sky, or a bird on the wing,
Or all of God's angels in heav'n for to sing,
He surely could have it, 'cause he was the King.

I wonder as I wander out under the sky,
How Jesus the Savior did come for to die
For poor on'ry people like you and like I . . .
I wonder as I wander out under the sky.

A PRAYER AS I REFLECT ON ALL THE PEOPLE YOU PLACED IN MY LIFE

Lord, I think about my family, my relatives, my neighbors, people with whom I will spend this day. Dear Jesus, as I look at their faces and remember their stories, there are feelings of gratitude and some fear and anxiety. Thank you for these loved ones, and please forgive me for the ways I have been less than accepting and loving. Please heal the wounds, divisions, and conflicts that stand between us and help me to remember how dearly you love them. I only want to remember that you have come to save us all. Amen.

FACTOIDS
In 1907, Oklahoma became the last US state to declare Christmas a legal holiday.

CHRISTMAS GREETINGS
from a Fairy to a Child

LEWIS CARROLL

Lady dear, if Fairies may
For a moment lay aside
Cunning tricks and elfish play,
'Tis at happy Christmas-tide.

We have heard the children say –
Gentle children, whom we love –
Long ago, on Christmas Day,
Came a message from above.

Still, as Christmas-tide comes round,
They remember it again —
Echo still the joyful sound
Peace on earth, good-will to men!"

Yet the hearts must childlike he
Where such heavenly guests abide:
Unto children, in their glee,
All the year is Christmas-tide!

Thus, forgetting tricks and play
For a moment, Lady dear,
We would wish you, if we may,
Merry Christmas, Glad New Year!

Traditions

CHRISTMAS TREES, TREE DECORATIONS

The Christmas tree, or historically, the *Tannenbaum*, is symbolic of peace and eternal life. The symbols connected to the tree and its decorations, which we have come to think of as traditional, are a wonderful meditation for Christians. However, this Christmas tradition also has its roots in ancient paganism. Let's take a quick look at the ancient pagan origins and work our way up to the more current traditions of Christmas trees and their Christian symbolism.

Ancient pagans used evergreens to celebrate the fact that eventually winter would be over, the evil spirits would recede to their usual practices, and life would begin again. Vikings in Northern Europe also saw evergreens as a symbol of hope that spring would return after a cold, dark winter. Druids in England and France decorated oak trees with fruit and candles to honor their gods of harvest and light. Romans decorated trees with trinkets and candles during Saturnalia, the midwinter harvest festival, and during the revelry of Mithras, the Persian god of light and truth. The common theme of life renewing after a cold, harsh winter holds true also for the ancient Egyptians. All of these cultures revered the evergreen trees for their refusal to die when everything else did, and they decorated them to celebrate their promise. This celebration of hope continued on into the Middle Ages with the Scandinavians and Germans.

There are several legends regarding Christmas trees, and several of them involve Martin Luther. Supposedly, in 1500 Martin Luther was walking through a forest on Christmas Eve where he spied a group of evergreens covered in snow and sparkling from the stars in the sky. He cut one down and took it home, decorating it with lit candles to replicate the trees he had found in the forest. His idea was to glorify Christ by the use of the candles to replicate the beauty of the stars reflected on the snow-covered boughs. The tree, pointing upward toward the heavens, inspired him to praise God.

In another legend, Saint Boniface, an English monk who organized the churches of Germany and France, stopped a pagan human sacrifice by slamming his fist into the sacred oak being used for that sacrifice. The tree was completely felled by that blow, and in its place grew a fir, which Saint Boniface said was the Tree of Life, representing eternal life in Christ.

Germans have a long history of decorating trees for Christmas, with the first historical mention of this practice coming from Strasburg, Germany, in 1605. They decorated with gold foil, apples, wafers, sweets, and paper roses. In the 1700s, as Germans emigrated to America, they brought with them the custom of the decorated tree. In the New World, they added to their usual decorations animal cookies, strings of popcorn, and brightly colored paper. In the 1890s Germany became a manufacturer of Christmas ornaments for America and England.

Puritans tried to hold the line against such practices as decorations by firing people who decorated trees or who missed work or school to celebrate Christmas Day. They banned Christmas in New England, and as late as 1851 a Cleveland minister nearly lost his job because he allowed a tree in his church. Despite all their efforts to discourage the celebration, the inevitable was accomplished by the early part of the twentieth century, and Christmas has been an established holiday for countless generations. After the invention of the electric bulb, community trees appeared all over North America, burning brightly for days on end.

Today, people in most parts of the Northern Hemisphere celebrate Christmas with trees. Evergreen trees are the most popular choice for decorating, although artificial trees appeal to a great number of people for the ease and convenience of using them. Artificial trees are now manufactured in the greatest variety of styles imaginable: aluminum, feathers, trees made to look like real evergreen trees, fiber optics, and as many sizes and shapes as the people who prefer them.

It's lovely to drive through the neighborhoods at night during the Christmas season and see the beautiful trees lit with brilliant, colored lights, and decorated with incredible ornaments that are amazing in their variety. A common placement of a Christmas tree is in front of a window so that it can be seen and enjoyed by everyone who passes by. A treatment that seems to be increasing in popularity is the decorating of trees and bushes in the yard, covered with blankets of lights or lit with lights spiraled along the branches. Many people make good use of being home the day after Thanksgiving to get these lights and decorations up so that they can enjoy a long season, often lasting into January.

To Christians the Christmas tree has a special meaning. It represents the cross on which Jesus died. With his death the bridge was made between life and death. The lights on the tree represent Christ as the Light of the world for whom he was willing to sacrifice himself. The ornaments represent believers — the fruit, the offspring of the union between Christ and his Church.

I SAW THREE SHIPS

The story of this carol begins with the Empress Helena, who commanded that the relics of the Magi be brought to Byzantium. These three skulls were eventually taken to Milan and then, in 1162, to Cologne.

According to folk tradition, the relics made their journey from Bethlehem to Cologne in three ships. As minstrels sang the tale, the destination changed, and so did the identity of the travelers. The result was a carol: "I saw three ships come sailing in, on Christmas Day, on Christmas Day. I saw three ships come sailing in, on Christmas Day in the morning." It asked, "And what was in those ships all three?" The answer was the Holy Family, or "Our Savior Christ and his lady." The carol asked, "And where they sailed those ships all three?" The obvious answer: "All they sailed in to Bethlehem." We may not understand the logic, but it worked for centuries of carolers in the pageants, processions, and parties during Christmas and the twelve-day season that followed.

I SAW THREE SHIPS

I saw three ships come sailing in
On Christmas Day, on Christmas Day;
I saw three ships come sailing in
On Christmas Day in the morning.

And what was in those ships all three,
On Christmas Day, on Christmas Day?
And what was in those ships all three,
On Christmas Day in the morning?

Our Savior Christ and his lady,
On Christmas Day, on Christmas Day;
Our Savior Christ and his lady,
On Christmas Day in the morning.

Pray, wither sailed those ships all three,
On Christmas Day, on Christmas Day;
Pray, wither sailed those ships all three,
On Christmas Day in the morning?

O they sailed into Bethlehem,
On Christmas Day, on Christmas Day;
O they sailed into Bethlehem,
On Christmas Day in the morning.

And all the bells on earth shall ring,
On Christmas Day, on Christmas Day;
And all the bells on earth shall ring,
On Christmas Day in the morning.

And all the Angels in Heaven shall sing,
On Christmas Day, on Christmas Day;
And all the Angels in Heaven shall sing,
On Christmas Day in the morning.

And all the souls on earth shall sing,
On Christmas Day, on Christmas Day;
And all the souls on earth shall sing,
On Christmas Day in the morning.

Then let us all rejoice again,
On Christmas Day, on Christmas Day;
Then let us all rejoice again,
On Christmas Day in the morning.

A PRAYER FOR MY SPOUSE ON CHRISTMAS MORNING

God of love, thank you for the gift you have given us in bringing us together. On this day when we celebrate the birth of your Son, may we take another step closer to each other in intimacy. With your guidance, we want to be more loving and thoughtful, less protective and defensive around each other. May we dedicate this day to renewing our love. As we leave the warmth of this bed to begin our day, bless us with the warmth of your great love for us and help us to remember to look for the light of your love in each other.
Amen.

TRIVIA
Christmas trees are edible. Many parts of pines, spruces and firs can be eaten. The needles are a good source of vitamin C. Pine nuts and pinecones are also good sources of nutrition.

CHRISTMAS CRAFTS AND HOMEMADE GIFTS

INEXPENSIVE WAYS TO CELEBRATE

Make Snowballs

Shape any flavor of ice cream into two-to-three-inch balls, quickly rolling each in coconut. Place balls on a cookie sheet and freeze. To serve, place one or two balls in a bowl. (If desired, you can put chocolate syrup in the bowl first.)

Create Unique Wrapping Paper

1. Use magazine pages to wrap small gifts.
2. Use the comic section of your newspaper as pretty paper.
3. Use your children's artwork, or create your own on plain paper.
4. Don't buy expensive ribbons and bows to decorate your packages; if you hunt around you can find the cheap stuff that will be just as pretty!
5. Forget the gift tags, make your own by cutting a small piece of matching paper and folding it in half. Write the "To and From" on the inside of the paper and tape it to the wrapped present. This is great for scraps of paper that are too small to wrap a gift but too large to toss away.
6. Cut up old Christmas cards for gift tags.
7. If you sew, use scrap material to wrap gifts.

Enjoy Entertainment

1. Instead of going to the theater, catch up on the DVDs that have come out for rental during the holiday season.

2. Get out the board games; the kids will love spending time with you. If you don't have many to choose from, borrow a new game from a friend or neighbor.

3. Playing cards is always fun too; even when the kids are little you can play Go Fish.

4. Sing, sing, sing! Many churches and groups even have caroling gatherings.

5. Tell on yourself a little. Sit around a warm fire, or cozy up in the living room with blankets and hot cocoa, and tell family stories.

6. Have a family gathering to decorate the tree or wrap presents.

7. Create a Christmas photo album of your favorite memories!

FOR FUN

OFFICE HOLIDAY MEMO

To: All employees
From: Management
Subject: Office conduct during the Christmas season

Effective immediately, employees should keep in mind the following guidelines in compliance with FROLIC (the Federal Revelry Office and Leisure Industry Council).

1. Running aluminum foil through the paper shredder to make tinsel is discouraged.
2. Playing "Jingle Bells" on the push-button phone is forbidden (it runs up an incredible long-distance bill).
3. Work requests are not to be filed under "Bah humbug."
4. Company cars are not to be used to go over the river and through the woods to Grandma's house.
5. All fruitcake is to be eaten BEFORE July 25.
6. Eggnog will NOT be dispensed in vending machines.

In spite of all this, the staff is encouraged to have a Happy Holiday.

CHRISTMAS IN INDIA

RUDYARD KIPLING

Dim dawn behind the tamarisks – the sky is saffron-yellow –
As the women in the village grind the corn,
And the parrots seek the riverside, each calling to his fellow
That the Day, the staring Easter Day is born.
Oh the white dust on the highway!
Oh the stenches in the byway!
Oh the clammy fog that hovers
And at Home they're making merry 'neath
the white and scarlet berry –
What part have India's exiles in their mirth?

Full day behind the tamarisks – the sky is blue and staring –
As the cattle crawl afield beneath the yoke,
And they bear One o'er the field –
path, who is past all hope or caring,
To the ghat below the curling wreaths of smoke.
Call on Rama, going slowly, as ye bear a brother lowly –
Call on Rama – he may hear, perhaps, your voice!
With our hymn-books and our psalters
we appeal to other altars,
And to-day we bid "good Christian men rejoice!"

High noon behind the tamarisks – the sun is hot above us –
As at Home the Christmas Day is breaking wan.
They will drink our healths at dinner –
those who tell us how they love us,

And forget us till another year he gone!
Oh the toil that knows no breaking!
Oh the Heimweh, ceaseless, aching!
Oh the black dividing Sea and alien Plain!
Youth was cheap — wherefore we sold it.
Gold was good — we hoped to hold it,
And today we know the fulness of our gain.

Grey dusk behind the tamarisks — the parrots fly together —
As the sun is sinking slowly over Home;
And his last ray seems to mock us shackled in a lifelong tether.
That drags us back how'er so far we roam.
Hard her service, poor her payment —
she is ancient, tattered raiment —
India, she the grim Stepmother of our kind.
if a year of life he lent her, if her temple's shrine we enter,
The door is shut — we may not look behind.

Black night behind the tamarisks —
the owls begin their chorus —
As the conches from the temple scream and bray.
With the fruitless years behind us,
and the hopeless years before us,
Let us honor, O my brother, Christmas Day!
Call a truce, then, to our labors —
Let us feast with friends and neighbors,
And be merry as the custom of our caste;
For if "faint and forced the laughter,"
and if sadness follow after,
We are richer by one mocking Christmas past.

CHRISTIANS AWAKE!
Salute the Happy Morn

This song was written by John Byrom as a Christmas present for his daughter, probably in 1749. Byrom was active in the evangelical revivals of the period and had both Charles and John Wesley as students and friends. The poem was first published as a broadside (a large sheet of paper on which ballads were customarily printed and which was sold like a newspaper) and set to an original tune by John Wainwright, an organist at the Manchester, England, Collegiate Church. Byrom first heard the completed hymn on Christmas Day, 1750, when a group of men and boys led by Wainwright sang it for him.

Christians, awake, salute the happy morn
Whereon the Savior of the world was born
Rise to adore the mystery of love
Which hosts of angels chanted from above
With them the joyful tidings first begun
Of God incarnate and the Virgin's son

Then to the watchful shepherds it was told
Who heard the angelic herald's voice: "Behold,
I bring good tidings of a Savior's birth
To you and all the nations upon earth
This day hath God fulfilled His promised word;
This day is born a Savior, Christ the Lord."

He spake, and straightaway the celestial choir
In hymns of joy, unknown before, conspire
The praises of redeeming love they sang
And heaven's whole orb with alleluias rang
God's highest glory was their anthem still
Peace upon earth and unto men goodwill

To Bethlehem straight the shepherds ran
To see the wonder God had wrought for man
And found, with Joseph and the blessed Maid
Her Son, the Savior, in a manger laid
Amazed, the wondrous story they proclaim
The earliest heralds of the Savior's name

Let us, like these good shepherds, them employ
Our grateful voices to proclaim the joy
Trace we the Babe, who bath retrieved our loss
From His poor manger to His bitter cross
Treading His steps, assisted by His grace
Till man's first heavenly state again takes place

Then may we hope, the angelic thrones among
To sing, redeemed, a glad triumphal song
He that was born upon this joyful day
Around us all His glory shall display
Saved by His love, incessant we shall sing
Of angels and of angel-men the King

FOR FUN

TOP 4 NOT-SO-TRADITIONAL CHRISTMAS ALBUMS OF ALL TIME

4. BOB RIVERS' TWISTED CHRISTMAS

How can you not like an album with such, um, classics as "Wreck The Malls," "O Come All Ye Grateful Dead-Heads," and "The Restroom Door Said Gentlemen"?

3. EVERYTHING I WANT FOR CHRISTMAS.

Push the chairs against the wall and kick back the rug — Big Bad Voodoo Daddy is going to swing you back to the holidays circa 1945! This is the one to get you burning off all those Christmas calories. Your dancin' feet won't resist!

2. DR. DEMENTO PRESENTS THE GREATEST CHRISTMAS NOVELTY CD.

The title says it all. Sixteen songs you know by heart — and maybe wish you didn't — including "Jingle Bells" barked by a pack of dogs, "All I Want For Christmas Is My Two Front Teeth" (Spike Jones and His City Slickers), and of course "The Chipmunk Song" by Alvin, Theodore, and Simon.

1. A CHARLIE BROWN CHRISTMAS.

The Vince Guaraldi Trio was a surprise choice in 1965 to provide the music for "A Charlie Brown Christmas" TV special. The network executives at first balked at a jazz trio scoring for a children's special. Soon they realized that the cartoon was a hit not only with children, but also with adults—and that the music fit the program perfectly. Great year round but especially at that most wonderful time of the year.

Christmas Around the World

RUSSIA

In Russia, the religious festival of Christinas is being replaced by the Festival of Winter, but in some parts of the country traditions are still maintained. In the traditional Russian Christmas, special prayers are said and people fast, sometimes for thirty-nine days, until January 6. On Christmas Eve, when the first evening star appears in the sky, families eat a twelve-course supper in honor of each of the twelve apostles.

On Christmas Day, hymns and carols are sung. People gather in churches, which have been decorated with the usual Christmas trees. Christmas dinner includes a variety of different meats, with goose and suckling pig being the favorites.

Babushka is a traditional Christmas figure who distributes presents to children. Her name means "Grandmother," and the legend is told that she declined to go with the wise men to see Jesus because of the cold weather. However, she regretted not going and tried to catch up, filling her basket with presents. She never found Jesus, and that is why she visits each house, leaving toys for good children.

The role of Father Christmas is played by *Dedushka Moroz,* or Grandfather Christmas.

Top 10 Things Wives Don't Want to Hear their Husbands Say on Christmas Day

1. *"You like it, hon? Almost look like real diamonds, don't they?"*
2. *"That cheese ball was for later?"*
3. *"I never imagined a deep-fried turkey would flame up like that."*
4. *"Timmy, why is Mommy's present hissing?"*
5. *"It's the thought that counts, right?"*
6. *"Hey, the game's about to start!"*
7. *"That's right, hon. Your own subscription to Guns & Ammo."*
8. *"Wow, thanks, Uncle Ted. Bagpipes!"*
9. *"It's two sizes smaller, darling — you know, for motivation."*
10. *"Well, if it isn't Roy and Angela and their seven kids — with suitcases! What a pleasant surprise!"*

FACTOIDS
It is estimated that 400,000 people become sick each year from eating tainted Christmas leftovers.

Christmas Around the World

I R A Q

In Christian homes, an unusual ceremony is held on Christmas Eve. In the house's courtyard, a child reads the story of the Nativity from an Arabic Bible; the other members of the family hold lighted candles. As soon as the story has been read, a bonfire of thorns is lit in one corner. The future of the house for the coming year depends upon the way the fire burns. If the thorns burn to ashes, the family will have good fortune. While the fire is burning, a psalm is sung.

When the fire is reduced to ashes, everyone jumps over the ashes three times and makes a wish.

On Christmas Day, a similar bonfire is built in the church. While the fire burns, the men of the congregation chant a hymn. This is followed by a procession in which church officials march behind the bishop, who carries an image of the infant Jesus upon a scarlet cushion. The long Christmas service always ends with the blessing of the people. The bishop reaches forth and touches a member of the congregation with his hand, putting his blessing upon him. That person touches the one next to him, and so on, until all have received the "Touch of Peace."

A PRAYER WHILE OPENING GIFTS

*Let me just for a moment, Lord, hold this time in my
heart. It is all out mysteries and gratitude, unknowing
and wrong sizes, snippets of ribbon and screams of
delight. Help me to remember the immense love you
have for each of us in this room. With each gift that is
opened, no matter how perfect or imperfect, let me feel
again the many ways you bless us each day, especially
with your presence in our hearts and the presence of
eacb other in our lives.*
Amen.

FACTOIDS

*In 1996, Christmas caroling was banned at two major
malls in Pensacola, Florida. Apparently, shoppers and
merchants complained that the carolers were too loud
and took up too much space.*

CHRISTMAS POEM

G. H. CHESTERTON

There fared a mother driven forth
Out of an inn to roam;
In the place where she was homeless
All men are at home.
The crazy stable close at hand,
With shaking timber and shifting sand,
Grew a stronger thing to abide and stand
Than the square stones of Rome.

For men are homesick in their homes,
And strangers under the sun,
And they lay their heads in a foreign land
Whenever the day is done.

Here we have battle and blazing eyes,
And chance and honor and high surprise,
But our homes are under miraculous skies
Where the yule tale was begun.

A child in a foul stable,
Where the beasts feed and foam;
Only where He was homeless
Are you and I at home;
We have hands that fashion and heads that know,
But our hearts we lost — how long ago!

In a place no chart nor ship can show
Under the sky's dome.

This world is wild as an old wife's tale,
And strange the plain things are,
The earth is enough and the air is enough
For our wonder and our war;
But our rest is as far as the fire-drake swings
And our peace is put in impossible things
Where clashed and thundered unthinkable wings
Round an incredible star.

To an open house in the evening
Home shall all men come,
To an older place than Eden
And a taller town than Rome.
To the end of the way of the wandering star,
To the things that cannot be and that are,
To the place where God was homeless
And all men are at home.

TRIVIA

The poem commonly referred to as "The Night Before
Christmas" was originally titled "A Visit from Saint
Nicholas." This poem was written by Clement Moore
for his children and some guests, one of whom
anonymously sent the poem to a New York newspaper
for publication.

BEN JONSON'S CAROL

BEN JONSON

The words of this lovely carol were written by the celebrated Elizabethan playwright Ben Jonson (1573-1637), a contemporary of William Shakespeare. Sir Arthur Sullivan composed the music, which is most associated with the hymn. Sir Arthur Seymour Sullivan was born in Lambeth, London, in 1842. A musical child prodigy, he composed his own anthem when he was just eight years old. He is best known for his famous collaboration with W. S. Gilbert (1836-1911) from 1871 to 1896, when they produced their fourteen much-loved comic operas.

> *I sing the birth was born tonight,*
> *The Author both of life and light:*
> *The angels so did sound it,*
> *The angels so did sound it, so did sound it;*
>
> *They like the ravished shepherds said,*
> *Who saw the light and were afraid,*
> *Yet searched, and true they found it,*
> *Yet searched, and true they found it,*
> *True they found it, and true they found it.*
>
> *The Son of God, the eternal King,*
> *That did us all salvation bring,*
> *And freed the world from danger,*
> *And freed the world from danger, freed from danger,*

He whom the whole world could not take,
the Word which heaven and earth did make,
Was now laid in a manger,
Was now laid in a manger
In a manger, laid in a manger.

What comfort do we by Him win,
Who made Himself the price of sin,
To make us heirs of glory!
To make us heirs of glory, heirs of glory!

To see this Babe, all innocence,
A Martyr's horn in our defense —
Can man forget the story,
Can man forget the story,
Forget the story? Can man forget the story?

FACTOIDS

In America, the weeks leading up to Christmas
are the biggest shopping weeks of the year.
Many retailers make up to 70 percent of their
annual revenue in the month preceding
Christmas.

A PRAYER FOR THOSE GOING TO WORK ON CHRISTMAS DAY

Loving God, on this sacred day I am going to work. There is something special about working on Christmas, when so many others are home with loved ones. My work today may even have a wondrous sense of service and necessity. But it doesn't always feel noble, and inside me there is a struggle: I wish I could stay home. Help me to feel commissioned by you today. Let me recognize the unique way my coworkers and I are called to serve our brothers and sisters. Let me take just a moment in this quiet to feel your deep love for me. May I carry that sense of peace with me as the light of your love, shining on everyone I come in contact with today. Thank you.

FOR FUN

In a small Southern town there was a "Nativity Scene" that showed great skill and talent had gone into creating it. One small feature bothered me.

The three wise men were wearing firemen's helmets. Totally unable to come up with a reason or explanation, I left. At a Qwik Stop on the edge of town, I asked the lady behind the counter about the helmets. She exploded into a rage, yelling at me, "You stupid Yankees never do read the Bible!" I assured her that I did, but simply couldn't recall anything about firemen in the Bible.

She jerked her Bible from behind the counter, ruffled through some pages, and finally jabbed her finger at a passage. Sticking it in my face she said, "See, it says right here, the three man came from afar."

TRIVIA

The first charity Christmas card was produced by UNICEF in 1949. The picture chosen for the card was painted not by a professional artist but by a seven-year-old girl. The girl was Jitka Samkova of Rudolfo, a small town in the former nation of Czechoslovakia. The town received UNICEF assistance after World War II, inspiring Jitka to paint some children dancing around a maypole. She said her picture represented "joy going round and round."

CHRISTMAS TREE
A Christmas Circular Letter

ROBERT FROST

The city had withdrawn into itself
And left at last the country to the country;
When between whirls of snow not come to lie
And whirls of foliage not yet laid, there drove
A stranger to our yard, who looked the city,
Yet did in country fashion in that there
He sat and waited till he drew us out
A-buttoning coats to ash him who he was.
He proved to be the city come again
To look for something it had left behind
And could not do without and keep its Christmas.
He asked if I would sell my Christmas trees;
My woods — the young fir balsams like a place
Where houses all are churches and have spires.
I hadn't thought of them as Christmas Trees.
I doubt if I was tempted for a moment
To sell them off their feet to go in cars
And leave the slope behind the house all bare,

Where the sun shines now no warmer than the moon.
I'd hate to have them know it if I was.
Yet more I'd hate to hold my trees except
As others hold theirs or refuse for them,
Beyond the time of profitable growth,
The trial by market everything must come to.
I dallied so much with the thought of selling.
Then whether from mistaken courtesy
And fear of seeming short of speech, or whether
From hope of hearing good of what was mine,
I said, "There aren't enough to be worth while."
"I could soon tell how many they would cut,
You could look them over."

"You could look.
But don't expect I'm going to let you have them."
Pasture they spring in, some in clumps too close
That lop each other of boughs, hut not a few
Quite solitary and having equal boughs
All round and round. The latter he nodded "Yes" to,
Or paused to say beneath some lovelier one,
With a buyer's moderation, "That would do."
I thought so too, but wasn't there to say so.
We climbed the pasture on the south, crossed over,
And came down on the north.
He said, "A thousand."

"A thousand Christmas trees! — at what apiece?"

He felt some need of softening that to me:
"A thousand trees would come to thirty dollars."

Then I was certain I had never meant
To let him have them. Never show surprise!
But thirty dollars seemed so small beside
The extent of pasture I should strip, three cents
(For that was all they figured out apiece),
Three cents so small beside the dollar friends
I should be writing to within the hour
Would pay in cities for good trees like those,
Regular vestry-trees whole Sunday Schools
Could hang enough on to pick off enough.
A thousand Christmas trees I didn't know I had!
Worth three cents more to give away than sell,
As may be shown by a simple calculation.
Too bad I couldn't lay one in a letter.
I can't help wishing I could send you one,
In wishing you herewith a Merry Christmas.

FOR FUN

TOP 10 WORST GIFTS TO GIVE YOUR TEENAGER

10. *School supplies*

9. *Pajamas*

8. *Underwear*

7. *Homemade "Hug" coupons*

6. *Clothing you think is really cute*

5. *Any clothing you pick out*

4. *The Best of Rodgers and Hammerstein CD set*

3. *Any music you pick out*

2. *Anything you pick out other than cash or gift cards*

1. *A gift card for the Needlepoint Exchange*

FACTOIDS
More diamonds are purchased at Christmastime (31 percent) than during any other holiday or occasion during the year.

Christmas Around the World

VENEZUELA

On December 16, families bring out their *pesebres*, which are specially designed depictions of the nativity scene.

It is customary in Venezuela to attend one of nine carol services. Firecrackers explode and bells ring to call worshippers from bed in the predawn hours. The last of the masses takes place on *Nochebuena de Navidad*, or Christmas Eve. Families attend mass and then return home to a large dinner.

On January 6, children awaken to discover that the straw they had left beside their bed is gone, and in its place are gifts left by the Magi and their camels. If they have a black smudge on their cheek, the children know that Balthazar, King of the Ethiopians, has kissed them while they slept.

CAROL OF THE BELLS

The original music for "Carol of the Bells," Shchedryk, actually celebrated the coming of spring, rather than Christmas. The lyrics described the view of birds sitting on the eaves of an inn. The choral work, written by Mykola Dmytrovich Leontovych, was first performed by students at Kiev University in December 1916.

The song became Christmas music in 1936 when Peter J. Wilhousky changed the main characters, so to speak, from birds to bells! Someone thought Wilhousky had a grand idea and came up with a slightly altered version.

So, how do you know if you're listening to the original or the copy? The first line will tell. If you hear "Hark! How the bells, sweet silver bells," you've got the original. However, if you hear "Hark to the bells, Hark to the bells," you're listening to the non-Wilhousky version.

CAROL OF THE BELLS

Hark! How the bells,
Sweet silver bells,
All seem to say,
"Throw cares away."

Christmas is here,
Bringing good cheer
To young and old,
Meek and the bold.

Ding, dong, ding, dong
That is their song,
With joyful ring,
All caroling.

One seems to hear
Words of good cheer
From everywhere,
Filling the air.

Oh, how they pound,
Raising the sound
O'er hill and dale,
Telling their tale.

Gaily they ring,
While people sing
Songs of good cheer,
Christmas is here!

Merry, merry, merry,
Merry Christmas,
Merry, merry, merry,
Merry Christmas.

On, on they send,
On without end
Their joyful tone
To every home.
Ding dong, ding dong

Hark to the Bells,
Hark to the Bells,
Telling us all
Jesus is King.

Strongly they chime,
Sound with a rhyme,
Christmas is here!
Welcome the King!

Hark to the Bells,
Hark to the Bells.
This is the day,
Day of the King.

A PRAYER BEFORE CHRISTMAS DINNER

God of all gifts, we thank you for the many ways you have blessed us this day. We are grateful for each of those who are gathered around this table. We ask you to bless us and our food and to bless those we love who are not with us today. In our gratitude and love, we remember the humble birth of your Son and pray for those who are without enough to eat. We remember the stable in which your Son was born, and we pray for those who have no place to live. We remember the challenging message of caring and giving preached by your Son, and we pray for peace in families and nations throughout the world.

We bless you and give you thanks for the gift of your Son, who was born on the first Christmas Day, and for your Spirit who brings our hearts to life on every Christmas Day, now and forever.

Amen.

TRIVIA

Frankincense is a sweet-smelling gum resin derived from certain Boswellia trees, which at the time of Christ grew in Arabia, India, and Ethiopia. Tradition says that it was presented to the Christ Child by Balthasar, the black king from Ethiopia or Saba. The frankincense trade was at its height during the days of the Roman Empire. At that time this resin was considered as valuable as gems or precious metals. The Romans burned frankincense on their altars and at cremations.

FOOD TRADITIONS

POLAND

The Polish word for Christmas Eve is *Wigilia* (pronounced VI-gee-lee-ah). Its root is like the English word vigil: waiting for Christ to be born. At the end of the *Wigilia* meal the family goes off to midnight mass at church. There are usually twelve dishes in a *Wigilia* meal to symbolize the twelve apostles, though some families serve thirteen. There is no fixed set of rules for what the twelve (or thirteen) dishes must be; the items in the meal change somewhat according to location and availability of ingredients. A traditional *Wigilia* meal may include: fish in horseradish sauce; pickled beets; pickled herring in sour cream; pierogi; stewed sauerkraut with mushrooms; Christmas Eve kutia; almond soup; noodles with poppyseed and raisins; poppyseed rolls; Christmas bread; baked apples with red wine; Marzipan twelve-fruit compote. (Approximate U.S. measurements.)

Polish Pike

INGREDIENTS:

fish fillets (carp, sole, pike, similar fish)
2 carrots
2 stalks celery
1 parsley root
1 onion, quartered
5 peppercorns
1 bay leaf
2 teaspoons salt
6 cups water

SAUCE:

1.75 ounces and 1 tablespoon butter
scant 1/4 cup flour
3/4 cup and 1 tablespoon prepared cream-style horseradish
1 teaspoon sugar
1/8 to 1/4 teaspoon salt
1/2 cup and 2 tablespoon sour cream
eggs, hard-cooked, peeled, and sieved

DIRECTIONS:

Combine vegetables, dry seasonings, and water in a saucepan or pot.

Bring to a boil; simmer 20 minutes, then strain. Cook fish in the strained vegetable stock 6 to 10 minutes, or until fish flakes easily. Remove fish from stock. Arrange on serving platter and cover with plastic wrap. Chill. Strain fish stock and reserve 3/4 cup for horseradish sauce; cool.

For horseradish sauce, melt the butter in a saucepan, then blend in flour until smooth, making a roux.

Add the cooked fish stock gradually, stirring constantly. Cook and stir until the sauce boils and becomes thick and smooth. Remove from heat and stir in horseradish, sugar, salt, sour cream, and, eggs. Cool for 15 minute

Pour the horseradish sauce over the chilled fish and garnish with shredded lettuce.

THE THREE KINGS

HENRY WADSWORTH LONGFELLOW

Three Kings came riding from far away,
Melchior and Gaspar and Baltasar;
Three Wise Men out of the East were they,
And they travelled by night and they slept by day,
For their guide was a beautiful, wonderful star.

The star was so beautiful, large and clear,
That all the other stars of the sky
Became a white mist in the atmosphere,
And by this they knew that the coming was near
Of the Prince foretold in the prophecy.

Three caskets they bore on their saddle-bows,
Three caskets of gold with golden keys;
Their robes were of crimson silk with rows
Of bells and pomegranates and furbelows,
Their turbans like blossoming almond-trees.

And so the Three Kings rode into the West,
Through the dusk of the night, over hill and dell,
And sometimes they nodded with beard on breast,
And sometimes talked, as they paused to rest,
With the people they met at some wayside well.

"Of the child that is born," said Balthasar,
"Good people, I pray you, tell us the news;
For we in the East have seen this star,
And have ridden fast, and have ridden far,
To find and worship the King of the Jews."

And the people answered, "You ask in vain;
We know of no King but Herod the Great!"
They thought the Wise Men were men insane,
As they spurred their horses across the plain,
Like riders in haste, who cannot wait.

And when they came to Jerusalem,
Herod the Great, who had heard this thing,
Sent for the Wise Men and questioned them;
And said, "Go down unto Bethlehem,
And bring me tidings of this new king."

So they rode away; and the star stood still,
The only one in the grey of morn;
Yes, it stopped — it stood still of its own free will,
Right over Bethlehem on the hill,
The city of David, where Christ was born.

And the Three Kings rode through the gate and the guard,
Through the silent street, till their horses turned
And neighed as they entered the great inn-yard;
But the windows were closed, and the doors were barred,
And only a light in the stable burned.

And cradled there in the scented hay,
In the air made sweet by the breath of kine,
The little child in the manger lay,
The child, that would he king one day
Of a kingdom not human, but divine.

His mother Mary of Nazareth
Sat watching beside his place of rest,
Watching the even flow of his breath,
For the joy of life and the terror of death
Were mingled together in her breast.

They laid their offerings at his feet:
The gold was their tribute to a King,
The frankincense, with its odor sweet,
Was for the Priest, the Paraclete,
The myrrh for the body's burying.

And the mother wondered and bowed her head,
And sat as still as a statue of stone,
Her heart was troubled yet comforted,
Remembering what the Angel had said
Of an endless reign and of David's throne.

Then the Kings rode out of the city gate,
With a clatter of hoofs in proud array;
But they went not back to Herod the Great,
For they knew his malice and feared his hate,
And returned to their homes by another way.

A CHRISTMAS CAROL

G. K CHESTERTON

The Christ-child lay on Mary's lap,
His hair was like a light.
(O weary, weary were the world,
But here is all aright.)

The Christ-child lay on Mary's breast
His hair was like a star.
(O stern and cunning are the kings,
But here the true hearts are.)

The Christ-child lay on Mary's heart,
His hair was like a fire.
(O weary, weary is the world,
But here the world's desire.)

The Christ-child stood on Mary's knee,
His hair was like a crown,
And all the flowers looked up at Him,
And all the stars looked down.

A PRAYER OF REFLECTION

Father God,
When your precious Son came to earth as a tiny
baby born in a stable in Bethlehem in poverty and
simplicity, you changed our world. As we imagine
those surroundings, we join with the shepherds and
the wise men in wonder and praise. We thank you
for our material lives, praise you for our spiritual
lives, and trust in you for our eternal life.
Amen.

TRIVIA
The carol "Silent Night" was written in 1818 by an
Austrian priest, Joseph Mohr. He was told the day
before Christmas that the church organ was broken and
would not be prepared in time for Christmas Eve. He
was saddened by this news and could not think of
Christmas without music, so he wanted to write a carol
that could be sung by choir to guitar music. He sat
down and wrote three stanzas. Later that night the
people in the little Austrian church sang "Stille Nacht"
for the first time.

THOU DIDST LEAVE THY THRONE

EMILY S. ELLIOT

Thou didst leave Thy throne and Thy kingly crown
When Thou earnest to earth for me;
But in Bethlehem's home was there found no room
For Thy holy nativity.
O come to my heart, Lord Jesus —
There is room in my heart for Thee.

Heaven's arches rang when the angels sang,
Proclaiming Thy royal degree;
But of lowly birth didst Thou come to earth,
And in great humility.
O come to my heart, Lord Jesus —
There is room in my heart for Thee.

The foxes found rest, and the birds their nest
In the shade of the forest tree;
But Thy couch was the sod, O Thou Son of God,
In the deserts of Galilee.
O come to my heart, Lord Jesus —
There is room in my heart for Thee.

Thou earnest, O Lord, with the living Word
That should set Thy people free;
But with mocking scorn and with crown of thorn,
They bore Thee to Calvary.
O come to my heart, Lord Jesus —
There is room in my heart for Thee.

When the heavens shall ring, and the angels sing,
At Thy coming to victory,
Let Thy voice call me home, saying "Yet there is room —
There is room at my side for Thee."
My heart shall rejoice, Lord Jesus,
When Thou comest and callest for me!

FOR FUN

THE CLAUS FAMILY

St. Nicholas is the main Claus. His wife is a relative Claus. His children are dependent Clauses. Their Dutch uncle is a restrictive Claus, As a group, they're all renown Clauses. Santa elves are subordinate Clauses.

SNOW STORM

RALPH WALDO EMERSON

Announced by all the trumpets of the sky,
Arrives the snow, and, driving o'er the fields,
Seems nowhere to alight: the whited air
Hides hills and woods, the river, and the heaven,
And veils the farm-house at the garden's end.
The sled and traveler stopped, the courier's feet
Delayed, all friends shut out, the housemates sit
Around the radiant fireplace, enclosed
In a tumultuous privacy of storm.
Come see the north wind's masonry.
Out of an unseen quarry evermore
Furnished with tile, the fierce artificer
Curves his white bastions with projected roof
Round every windware stake, or tree, or door.
Speeding, the myriad-handed, his wild work
So fanciful, so savage, nought cares he
For number or proportion. Mockingly,
On coop or kennel he hangs Parian wreaths;
A swan-like form invests the hidden thorn;

Fills up the farmer's lane from wall to wall,
Maugre the farmer's sighs; and at the gate
A tapering turret overtops the work.
And when his hours are numbered, and the world
Is all his own, retiring, as he were not,
Leaves, when the sun appears, astonished Art
To mimic in slow structures, stone by stone,
Built in an age, the mad wind's night-work,
The frolic architecture of the snow.

OF THE FATHERS LOVE BEGOTTEN

AURELIUS C. PRUDENTIUS, FOURTH CENTURY

Translated by John M. Neale, 1854, and Henry W. Baker. 1859

Of the Fathers love begotten,
Ere the worlds began to be,
He is Alpha and Omega,
He the Source, the Ending he,
Of the things that are,
that have been,
And that future years shall see,
Evermore and evermore!

O that birth forever blessed,
When the Virgin, full of grace,
By the Holy Ghost conceiving,
Bare the Savior of our race;
And the Babe,
the world's Redeemer,
First revealed his sacred face,
Evermore and evermore!

O ye heights of heav'n,
adore him;
Angel hosts, his praises sing,
Pow'rs, dominions,
bow before him,
And extol our God and King;
Let no tongue on earth be silent,
Every voice in concert ring,
Evermore and evermore!

Christ, to thee with
God the Father,
And, O Holy Ghost, to thee,
Hymns and chant
and high thanksgiving
And unwearied praises be:
Honor, glory, and dominion,
And eternal victory,
Evermore and evermore!

A PRAYER FOR THE FAMILY

*O God, bless our family and all its members
and friends; bind us together by your love. Give
us kindness and patience to support each other,
and wisdom in all we do.
Let the gift of your peace come into our hearts
and remain with us. May we rejoice in your
blessings for all our days. Amen.*

FACTOIDS

*In Sweden, a common Christmas decoration is
the Julbock. Made from straw, it is a small
figure of a goat. A variety of straw decorations
are a usual feature of Scandinavian Christmas
festivities.*

THE BELLS

EDGAR ALLAN POE

Hear the sledges with the bells — Silver Bells!
What a world of merriment their melody foretells!
How they tinkle, tinkle, tinkle, In the icy air of night!
While the stars that oversprinkle
All the heavens seem to twinkle
With a crystalline delight;
Keeping time, time, time,
In a sort of Runic rhyme,
To the tintinnabulation that so musically wells
From the bells, bells, bells, bells,
Bells, bells, bells —
From the jingling and tinkling of the bells.

TRIVIA

George Washington spent Christmas night 1776 crossing the Delaware River in dreadful conditions. During Christmas 1777 he fared little better. At Valley Forge, Washington and his men had a miserable Christmas dinner of fowl cooked in a broth of turnips, cabbages, and potatoes.

THE HOLY NIGHT

ELIZABETH BARRETT BROWNING

We sat among the stalls at Bethlehem;
The dumb kine from their fodder turning them,
Softened their horn'd faces,
To almost human gazes
Toward the newly Born:
The simple shepherds from the star-lit brooks
Brought visionary looks,
As yet in their astonished hearing rung
The strange sweet angel-tongue:
The magi of the East, in sandals worn,
Knelt reverent, sweeping round,
With long pale beards, their gifts upon the ground,
The incense, myrrh, and gold
These baby hands were impotent to hold:
So let all earthlies and celestials wait
Upon thy royal state.
Sleep, sleep, my kingly One!

SOME CHILDREN SEE HIM

ALFRED BURT

Some children see Him lily white
The infant Jesus born this night
Some children see Him lily white
With tresses soft and fair!

Some children see Him bronzed and brown
the Lord of heav'n to earth come down
Some children see Him bronzed and brown
with dark and heavy hair (with dark and heavy hair!)

Some children see Him almond-eyed
This Savior whom we kneel beside
Some children see Him almond-eyed
With skin of yellow hue!

Some children see Him dark as they
Sweet Mary's Son to whom we pray
Some children see Him dark as they
And, ah! they love Him so!

The children in each different place
Will see the Baby Jesus' face
Like theirs but bright with heav'nly grace
And filled with holy light!

O lay aside each earthly thing
and with thy heart as offering
Come worship now the infant King
'tis love that's born tonight!

FOOD TRADITIONS

POLAND

Pierogi or Uszka

INGREDIENTS:

Dough

14 ounces flour
1 egg
pinch of salt
lukewarm water

DIRECTIONS:

On a pastry board mix flour, egg, and salt, slowly adding water and kneading. The dough is ready if it does not stick to the hand or pastry board. Divide dough into four parts and roll each one out thinly. With a wine glass cut out circles that are 2 to 2.5 inches in diameter. (For Uszka, cut out small squares.)

Place a teaspoon of the filling on each circle, fold over, and press the edges firmly. Cook for 5 minutes.

SAUERKRAUT AND MUSHROOM PIEROGI FILLINGS (KAPUSTA Z GRZYBAMI – NADZIENIE)

INGREDIENTS:

2 cups sauerkraut
1 cup mushrooms, chopped
1 onion, chopped
butter
salt
pepper

DIRECTIONS:

Cook sauerkraut for 10 minutes. Drain and chop well. Fry onion and mushrooms in butter, add sauerkraut, and fry until flavors are blended. Cool and fill dough circles.

POTATO FILLING (RUSKIE PIEROGI):

Put 1 pound of cooked potatoes and 6 ounces of cottage cheese through a meat grinder. Add 1 small raw egg along with 1 medium onion, finely chopped and browned to golden brown. Add salt and pepper.

CHEESE FILLING (PIEROGI Z SEREM):

Rub 1 pound of well-drained cottage cheese through a wire sieve, then mix thoroughly with 1 small egg (raw) and salt. The filling swells during cooking, so do not use too much. Serve immediately, after pouring butter over them.

O HOLY NIGHT

PLACIDE CLAPPEAU

O holy night, the stars are brightly shining;
It is the night of the dear Savior's birth;
Long lay the world in sin and error pining,
Till he appeared and the soul felt its worth.
A thrill of hope, the weary world rejoices,
For yonder breaks a new and glorious morn!
Fall on your knees!
O hear the angel voices!
O night divine!
O night when Christ was horn!
O night divine! O night divine!
O night, O night divine.

Led by the light of Faith serenely beaming,
With glowing hearts by his cradle we stand;
So led by light of a star sweetly gleaming,
Here came the Wise Men from Orient land.
The King of kings lay thus in lowly manger,
In all our trials born to be our Friend;

He knows our need;
He guards us from all danger,
Behold your King!
Before him lowly bend!
Behold your King!
Before him lowly bend!

Truly he taught us to love one another;
His law is Love and his gospel is Peace;
Chains shall he break, for the slave is our brother,
And in his Name, all oppression shall cease.
With hymns of joy in grateful chorus raising,
Let every heart adore his holy Name!
Christ is the Lord!
With saint and seraph praising,
His pow'r and glory evermore proclaim!
His pow'r and glory evermore proclaim!

The words to "O Holy Night" were written by Placide Clappeau in 1847. Clappeau was a wine merchant and mayor of Roquemaure, who wrote poems for his own enjoyment. It was translated from French to English by Unitarian minister John Sullivan Dwight (1812-1893).

Dwight's writing is valued by musicologists because he was the only one who chronicled the development of music through the New England states at the time of the Civil War.

At the time of its publication, the carol was not well received. Church authorities denounced it for lack of musical taste and "total absence of the spirit of religion." In spite of its early rejection, "O Holy Night" has become one of the most beloved Christmas carols sung each year.

SWEET LITTLE JESUS BOY

CHRISTINA ROSSETTI

Sweet little Jesus Boy,
They made you be born
In a manger
Sweet little Holy Child,
They didn't know who you was

Didn't know you come
To save us, Lord;
To take our sins away.
Our eyes was blind,
We couldn't see,
We didn't know who you was.

Long time ago,
You was born.
Born in a manger low,
Sweet little Jesus Boy.

The world treat you mean, Lord;
Treat me mean, too.
But that's how things
is down here,
We didn't know 'twas you

You done sword us how,
we is trying.
Master, you done showed
Us how,
Even when you's dying.

Just seem like we
Can't do right,
Look how we treated you.
But please sir,
Forgive us lord,
We didn't know 'twas you.

Sweet little Jesus Boy,
Born long time ago.
Sweet little Holy Child,
And we didn't
Know who you was.

MINSTRELS

WILLIAM WORDSWORTH

*The minstrels played their Christmas tune
Tonight beneath my cottage-eaves;
While, smitten by a lofty moon,
The encircling laurels, thick with leaves,
Gave back a rich and dazzling sheen,
That overpowered their natural green.*

*Through hill and valley every breeze
Had sunk to rest with folded wings:
Keen was the air, but could not freeze,
Nor check, the music of the strings;
So stout and hardy were the band
That scraped the chords with strenuous hand.*

*And who but listened? – till was paid
Respect to every inmate's claim,
The greeting given, the music played
In honor of each household name,
Duly pronounced with lusty call,
And "Merry Christmas" wished to all.*

GENTLY MARY LAID HER CHILD

JOSEPH S. COOK, 1919

Gently Mary laid her Child
Lowly in a manger;
There He lay, the undefiled,
To the world a Stranger:
Such a Babe in such a place,
Can He be the Savior?
Ask the saved of all the race
Who have found His favor.

Angels sang about His birth;
Wise men sought and found Him;
Heaven's star shone brightly forth,
Glory all around Him:
Shepherds saw the wondrous sight,
Heard the angels singing;
All the plains were lit that night,
All the hills were ringing.

Gentle Mary laid her Child
Lowly in a manger;
He is still the undefiled,
But no more a stranger:
Son of God, of humble birth,
Beautiful the story;
Praise His Name in all the earth,
Hail the King of glory.

Christmas Around the World

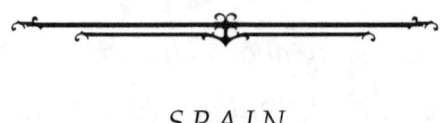

SPAIN

The Christmas season officially begins December 8 with the feast of the Immaculate Conception. It is celebrated each year in front of the great Gothic cathedral in Seville with a ceremony called *los Seises* or the dance of six. Oddly, the ritual dance is now performed by not six but ten elaborately costumed boys. It is a series of precise movements and gestures.

Most homes have a nativity scene complete with carved figures. During the weeks before Christmas, families gather around it to sing while children play tambourines and dance. The Spanish especially honor the cow at Christmas because it is thought that when Mary gave birth to Jesus, the cow in the stable breathed on the Baby Jesus to keep him warm.

On Christmas Eve, known as *Nochebuena*, or "the good night," is a time for family members to gather together. A traditional Christmas treat is *turron*, a kind of almond candy. As the stars come out, tiny oil lamps are lit in every house, and after midnight mass and Christmas dinner, streets fill with dancers and onlookers.

The Spanish Christmas is Navidad. People go to church, exchange presents, and many play on swing sets set up especially for the occasion. Swinging at solstice time evokes an ancient desire to encourage the sun, urging it to "swing" ever higher in the sky.

December 28 is the Feast of the Holy Innocents. Young boys of the town light bonfires, and one of them acts as the mayor.

He orders townspeople to perform civic chores such as sweeping the streets. Refusal to comply results in fines that are used to pay for the celebration.

Children think of the three wise men as the gift bearers. Tradition has it that they arrive on January 6.

Children fill their shoes with straw or barley for the tired camels that must carry their riders through the busy night. By morning the camel food is gone, and in its place are presents.

OUR CHRISTMAS MEMORIES AND TRADITIONS

A MEMORABLE YEAR _____

MEMORIES OF THE PAST YEAR

_____
_____
_____
_____
_____
_____
_____
_____
_____

WE GATHERED FOR THE HOLIDAYS AT

_____
_____
_____
_____

TRADITIONS AND SPECIAL EVENTS

_____

_____

_____

_____

_____

_____

_____

_____

_____

_____

_____

_____

_____

_____

THOSE WHO JOINED IN THE CELEBRATIONS

_____

_____

_____

_____

_____

_____

_____

OUR CHRISTMAS MEMORIES AND TRADITIONS

A MEMORABLE YEAR _____

MEMORIES OF THE PAST YEAR

_____

_____

_____

_____

_____

_____

_____

_____

_____

_____

WE GATHERED FOR THE HOLIDAYS AT

_____

_____

_____

_____

TRADITIONS AND SPECIAL EVENTS

_____
_____
_____
_____
_____
_____
_____
_____
_____
_____
_____
_____
_____
_____
_____

THOSE WHO JOINED IN THE CELEBRATIONS

_____
_____
_____
_____
_____
_____
_____

OUR CHRISTMAS MEMORIES AND TRADITIONS

A MEMORABLE YEAR _____

MEMORIES OF THE PAST YEAR

_____
_____
_____
_____
_____
_____
_____
_____
_____

WE GATHERED FOR THE HOLIDAYS AT

_____
_____
_____
_____

TRADITIONS AND SPECIAL EVENTS

_____

_____

_____

_____

_____

_____

_____

_____

_____

_____

_____

_____

_____

_____

_____

_____

_____

_____

THOSE WHO JOINED IN THE CELEBRATIONS

_____

_____

_____

_____

_____

_____

_____

_____

OUR CHRISTMAS MEMORIES AND TRADITIONS

A MEMORABLE YEAR _____

MEMORIES OF THE PAST YEAR

_____
_____
_____
_____
_____
_____
_____
_____
_____
_____
_____

WE GATHERED FOR THE HOLIDAYS AT

_____
_____
_____
_____

TRADITIONS AND SPECIAL EVENTS

_____

_____

_____

_____

_____

_____

_____

_____

_____

_____

_____

_____

_____

THOSE WHO JOINED IN THE CELEBRATIONS

_____

_____

_____

_____

_____

_____

_____

SECTION 3

Reflections on the Meaning of Christmas

THE GIFT OF GIFTS

*As each one has received a gift, minister it to one
another, as good stewards of the manifold grace of God.*
1 PETER 4:10 NKJV

Our first Christmas gift is the Gift of gifts, Jesus himself, the Son of God. Without Christ there is no Christmas, for a Christmas without Christ is meaningless. But the tiny babe in the crib has conquered all hearts. His birthday has become a day of joy for the whole world. It is not difficult to see, therefore, why events which fell on this birthday or happenings related to the sacred festival are of intense interest to every lover of the Christ Child.

How can we explain the mysterious fascination that hovers over every Christmas season? Is it not that all men inherently sense that Jesus continues to show the gifts of his grace on all mankind?

The antiphon of the Magnificat for the second vespers of Christmas Day best expresses the joy in our hearts:

"This day Christ is born; this day the Savior hath appeared; this day the angels sing on earth, the archangels rejoice; this day the just exult, saying: Glory to God in the highest, alleluia."

FACTOIDS
*In Syria, Christmas gifts are distributed by one of the
wise men's camels. The gift-giving camel is said to have
been the smallest one in the wise men's caravan.*

IN BETHLEHEM

Consider the wonderful truth of the prophets' words,
then the light will dawn in your souls and Christ the
Morning Star will shine in your hearts.
2 PETER 1:19 TLB

One Christmas Eve by torchlight, Saint Francis read aloud the story of the birth of Jesus. As the townspeople gathered, he read to them of the shepherds and the angels' song. He then spoke to them as a father might speak to his own children, telling them of love that is as gentle as a little child and willing to be poor and humble, as was the baby who lay in a manger among the cattle.

Brother Francis begged his listeners to put anger and hatred and envy out of their hearts and think only thoughts of peace and goodwill.

All listened eagerly while Brother Francis spoke, but the moment he finished, the great crowd broke into singing. Never before had such glorious hymns nor such joyous shouting been heard in the town of Greccio.

Only the mothers with babes in their arms and the shepherds in their woolly coats looked on silently and thought: "We are in Bethlehem."

TRIVIA

In many countries of the British Commonwealth, the day after
Christmas, December 26, is known as Boxing Day. It is also the
holy day called The Feast of Saint Stephen. The Stephen for whom
the day is named is the one in the Bible (Acts 6 – 8), who was the
first Christian to he martyred for his faith.

THE LONG-AWAITED MESSIAH

ANCIENT PROPHECIES FULFILLED BY THE CHRISTMAS CHILD

PROPHECY: Messiah Will Be Preceded by a Messenger

The voice of him that crieth in the wilderness, Prepare ye the way of the Lord, make straight in the desert a highway for our God (Isaiah 40:3 KJV).

JESUS:

In those days came John the Baptist, preaching in the wilderness of Judaea, and saying. Repent ye: for the kingdom of heaven is at hand (Matthew 3:1-2 KJV).

PROPHECY: He Will Be Born of a Virgin

Therefore the Lord himself shall give you a sign; Behold, a virgin shall conceive, and bear a son, and shall call his name Immanuel (Isaiah 7:14 KJV).

JESUS:

Now the birth of Jesus Christ was as follows: After His mother Mary was betrothed to Joseph, before they came together, she was found with child of the Holy Spirit (Matthew 1:18 NKJV).

PROPHECY: He Will Be a Descendant of King David

Behold, the days come, saith the Lord, that I will raise unto David a righteous Branch, and a King shall reign and prosper, and shall execute judgment and justice in the earth (Jeremiah 23:5 KJV).

JESUS:

And Joseph also went up from Galilee, out of the city of Nazareth, into Judea, unto the city of David, which is called Bethlehem; (because he was of the house and lineage of David) (Luke 2:4 KJV).

PROPHECY: He Will Be Born in Bethlehem

But thou, Bethlehem Ephratah, though thou be little among the thousands of Judah, yet out of thee shall he come forth unto me that is to be ruler in Israel; whose goings forth have been from of old, from everlasting (Micah 5:2 KJV).

JESUS:

Now when Jesus was born in Bethlehem of Judea in the days of Herod the king, behold, there came wise men from the east to Jerusalem (Matthew 2:1 KJV).

PROPHECY: Kings Will Bring Him Gifts

The kings of Tarshish and of the isles shall bring presents: the kings of Sheba and Seba shall offer gifts (Psalm 72:10 KJV).

JESUS:

Now when Jesus was born in Bethlehem of Judea . . . there came wise men from the east to Jerusalem . . . And when they were come into the house, they saw the young child with Mary his mother, and fell down, and worshipped him: and when they had opened their treasures, they presented unto him gifts; gold, and frankincense and myrrh. (Matthew 2:1, 11 KJV)

PROPHECY: He Will Be Called Out of Egypt

When Israel was a child, then I loved him, and called my son out of Egypt (Hosea 11:1 KJV).

JESUS:

And when they were departed, behold, the angel of the Lord appeareth to Joseph in a dream, saying, Arise, and take the young child and his mother, and flee into Egypt, and be thou there until I bring thee word: for Herod will seek the young child to destroy him. When he arose, he took the young child and his mother by night, and departed into Egypt: And was there until the death of Herod: that it might be fulfilled which was spoken of the Lord by the prophet, saying, Out of Egypt have I called my son (Matthew 2:13-15 KJV).

PROPHECY: His Own People Will Reject Him

He is despised and rejected of men; a man of sorrows, and acquainted with grief: and we hid as it were our faces from him; he was despised, and we esteemed him not (Isaiah 53:3 KJV). The stone which the builders rejected has become the chief cornerstone (Psalm 118:22 NASB).

JESUS:

He came to His own, and those who were His own did not receive Him. But as many as received Him. to them He gave the right to become children of God, even to those who believe in His name (John 1:11-12 NASB).

PROPHECY: Messiah Will Be Accused by False Witnesses

False witnesses did rise up; they laid to my charge things that I knew not. They rewarded me evil for good (Psalm 35:11-12 KJV).

JESUS:

Now the chief priests, and elders, and all the council, sought false witness against Jesus, to put him to death; but found none: yea, though many false witnesses came, yet found they none. At the last came two false witnesses (Matthew 26:59-60 KJV).

PROPHECY: Messiah Will Be a Light to the Gentiles

I will also give thee for a light to the Gentiles, that thou mayest be my salvation unto the end of the earth (Isaiah 49:6 KJV).

JESUS:

For mine eyes have seen thy salvation, which thou hast prepared before the face of all people; a light to lighten the Gentiles, and the glory of thy people Israel (Luke 2:30-32 KJV).

For so hath the Lord commanded us, saying, I have set thee to be a light of the Gentiles, that thou shouldest be for salvation unto the ends of the earth. And when the Gentiles heard this, they were glad, and glorified the word of the Lord: and as many as were ordained to eternal life believed (Acts 13:47-48 KJV).

PROPHECY: He Will Be Wounded and Bruised

But he was wounded for our transgressions, he was bruised for our iniquities: the chastisement of our peace was upon him; and with his stripes we are healed (Isaiah 53:5 KJV).

JESUS:

Then Pilate therefore took Jesus, and scourged him. And the soldiers platted a crown of thorns, and put it on his head, and they put on him a purple robe, and said, "Hail, King of the Jews!" and they smote him with their hands (John 19:1-3 KJV).

PROPHECY: The Messiah Will Die for Our Sins

Surely he hath borne our griefs, and carried our sorrows: yet we did esteem him stricken, smitten of God, and afflicted. But he was wounded for our transgressions, he was bruised for our iniquities: the chastisement of our peace was upon him; and with his stripes we are healed. All we like sheep have gone astray; we have turned every one to his own way; and the Lord hath laid on him the iniquity of us all (Isaiah 53:4-6 KJV).

JESUS:

God demonstrates His own love toward us, in that while we were yet sinners, Christ died for us (Romans 5:8 NASB).

PROPHECY: He Will Die by Crucifixion

I am poured out like water, and all my bones are out of joint. My heart has turned to wax; it has melted away within me. My strength is dried up like a potsherd, and my tongue sticks to the roof of my mouth; you lay me in the dust of death. Dogs have surrounded me; a band of evil men has encircled me, they have pierced my hands and my feet. I can count all my bones; people stare and gloat over me (Psalm 22:14-18).

EDITOR'S NOTE: Psalm 22:14-18 is a prophetic description of crucifixion, a brutal means of execution which would not be known until Roman times, approximately 1000 years after this prophecy.

JESUS:

And when they were come to the place, which is called Calvary, there they crucified him (Luke 23:33 KJV).

PROPHECY: They Will Gamble for His Clothing

They divide my garments among them, and for my clothing they cast lots (Psalm 22:18 NASB).

JESUS:

And they parted his raiment, and cast lots (Luke 23:34 KJV).

PROPHECY: He Will Be Buried in a Rich Man's Tomb

And he made his grave with the wicked, and with the rich in his death; because he had done no violence, neither was any deceit in his mouth (Isaiah 53:9 KJV).

JESUS:

When the even was come, there came a rich man of Arimathaea, named Joseph, who also himself was Jesus' disciple: He went to Pilate, and begged the body of Jesus. Then Pilate commanded the body to be delivered. And when Joseph had taken the body, he wrapped it in a clean linen cloth, and laid it in his own new tomb, which he had hewn out in the rock: and he rolled a great stone to the door of the sepulcher, and departed (Matthew 27:57-60 KJV).

PROPHECY: He Will Rise from the Dead

For thou wilt not leave my soul in hell; neither wilt thou suffer thine Holy One to see corruption (Psalm 16:10 KJV).

JESUS:

Christ died for our sins . . . He was buried . . . He was raised on the third day according to the Scriptures . . . He appeared to Cephas, then to the twelve. After that He appeared to more than five hundred (1 Corinthians 15:3-6 NASB).

FOR FUN

A CHRISTMAS PRAYER TO GRANDMA

Two young boys were spending the night at their grandparents. At bedtime, the two boys knelt beside the bed to say their prayers when the youngest one began praying at the top of his lungs . . .

*"I PRAY FOR A NEW BICYCLE . . .
I PRAY FOR A NEW XBOX . . .
I PRAY FOR A NEW LAPTOP . . ."*

*His older brother leaned over, nudged the younger brother, and said, "Why are you shouting your prayers? God isn't deaf."
To which the brother replied, "No, but Grandma is!"*

CHRISTMAS CRAFTS AND HOMEMADE GIFTS

FIVE PRICELESS GIFTS OF LOVE

The Gift of Compassion

We can make others feel cared for with the gift of compassion by listening with our heart, by seeking to understand with our mind, and by accepting rather than judging or correcting. Compassion speaks acceptance and understanding

The Gift of Courage

We must learn to be real with those we love, to become courageous in our communication. It starts with being truthful and honest with ourselves and with others, confronting unacceptable behavior, and remaining willing to work through issues. Courage brings peace and understanding when coupled with compassion. When we model courage, we provide opportunities for our loved ones to face the truth and learn to be courageous too.

The Gift of Service

Helping others fills the heart and soul in ways that nothing else can. As children see their parents help others, they discover the great joy and fulfillment that comes from giving. One of the best gifts we can give to our family is the gift of service.

The Gift of Creativity

Providing our family with many ways of expressing their creativity is a great gift. Creativity can be expressed in so many ways —cooking, crafts, handiwork, music, art, movement, storytelling, writing, humor, and photography! Creative family projects are especially wonderful in creating family closeness.

The Gift of Cheer

Cheerfulness is infectious. Laughter and playfulness can alleviate stress. Children enjoy their parents when they are playful, fun-loving, and joyful. Laughing together as a family is one of the most precious experiences in life.

OH, CHRISTMAS TREE!

Let the trees in the woods sing for joy before the Lord.
1 CHRONICLES 16:33 TLB

According to an ancient folktale, St. Boniface (St. Winifred) was preaching Christianity to the people of Germany one Christmas Eve, when he came upon a group of people standing around a huge oak tree. He was horrified to see that the group was preparing to offer a human sacrifice according to the Druid rites of the pagans.

In anger St. Boniface bravely felled the oak tree, and a tall young fir tree appeared in its place. Seeing this, he said to the people, "This new tree is unstained by blood. See how it points to the sky? You are to call it the tree of the Christ Child. Take it up and carry it into the castle of your chief.

"No longer shall you observe your secret and wicked rites in the shadow of the forest, but you shall hold ceremonies in your own homes that speak the message of peace and goodwill to all.

"A day is coming when every home in the land will celebrate the birthday of Christ by gathering around a fir tree in memory of this day and to the glory of God."

FACTOIDS
An average household in America will mail out twenty-
eight Christmas cards each year and see eight cards
return in their place.

Traditions

8 FAVORITE CHRISTMAS TREES

This list contains many people's top picks for Christmas trees. Scent, subtleties of needle color, and planting information is all here.

SCOTCH PINE

A classic conical shape and excellent needle retention make *Pinus sylvestris* the most popular cut tree of the holidays. It's also easy to grow because it tolerates a wide range of climates and soils.

NOBLE FIT

With its cool blue green, well-spaced branches and densely set, upwardly curved needles, *Abies nobilis* is aptly named. It's most often a cut tree, since it grows happily only in its Pacific Northwest home.

DOUGLAS FIT

Boasting a pyramidal shape and blunt, blue-to-dark-green needles, *Pseudotsuga menziesii* is a dependably long-lived cut tree. It flourishes in mild, humid climates with dry summers.

EASTERN WHITE PINE

Soft green color, long needles, and rich fragrance make *Pinus strobus* worthy of yuletide focus. Adaptable, fast growing, and moisture loving, it produces long, decorative pinecones.

GRAND FIR

With bicolor needles — deep green on top, white striped underneath —
Abies grandis makes a rich foil for ornaments. It grows well where
winters are long, summers are cool, and the air is humid and pristine.

VIRGINIA PINE

One of the few evergreens to tolerate warm winter temperatures,
Pinus virginiana is a first pick among Christmas trees for southerners.
It's also a good cut tree because, like all pines, it holds its needles well.

FRASER FIR

A regal, richly fragrant native tree, *Abies fraseri* has bicolor needles —
deep green on top, silvery-white below. Its generally slender profile
suits small rooms. Grow it only in cold-winter, cool-summer climates.

EASTERN RED CEDAR

Native to the eastern half of the United States. *Juniperus virginiana*
makes a cut or living tree with homespun appeal and pungent
fragrance. In the landscape, it tolerates drought, wind, and cold.

FOR FUN
*I once bought my kids a set of batteries for Christmas
with a note on it saying, toys not included.*
BERNARD MANNING

JOY TO THE WORLD PSALM

*O sing unto the Lord a new song; for he hath done
marvelous things: his right hand, and his holy arm,
hath gotten him the victory.
The Lord hath made known his salvation: his
righteousness hath he openly shewed in the sight of the
heathen.
He hath remembered his mercy and his truth toward
the house of Israel: all the ends of the earth have seen
the salvation of our God.
Make a joyful noise unto the Lord, all the earth: make a
loud noise, and rejoice, and sing praise.
Sing unto the Lord with the harp; with the harp, and
the voice of a psalm.
With trumpets and sound of cornet make a joyful noise
before the Lord, the King.
Let the sea roar, and the fullness thereof; the world, and
they that dwell therein.
Let the floods clap their hands: let the hills be joyful
together
Before the Lord; for he cometh to judge the earth: with
righteousness shall he judge the world, and the people
with equity.*

PSALM 98:1-9 KJV

FORGIVE US OUR CHRISTMASES

The story has been published of a little girl caught in the pre-Christmas swirl of activity, all of which seemed to be coming to a head on Christmas Eve. Dad, loaded down with bundles, seemed to have an even greater number of worries. Mom, under the pressure of getting ready for the great occasion, had yielded to tears several times during the day. The little girl herself, trying to help, found that she was always under foot, and sometimes adult kindness to her wore thin.

Finally, near tears herself, she was hustled off to bed. There kneeling to pray the Lord's Prayer before finally tumbling in, her mind and tongue betrayed her and she prayed, "Forgive us our Christmases as we forgive those who Christmas against us."

Perhaps the little girl's prayer was not such a great mistake. Too often we leave out the Christ of Christmas. Too often he is crowded out of our busy lives. Remember, the best gift won't be found in a box but in a person.

TRIVIA

Frustrated at the lack of interest in his new toy invention, Charles Pajeau hired several midgets, dressed them in elf costumes, and had them play with "Tinker Toys" in a display window at a Chicago department store during the Christmas season in 1914. This publicity stunt made the construction toy an instant hit. A year later, over a million sets of Tinker Toys had been sold.

FACTOIDS

In France, Christmas is called Noel. This is derived from the French phrase le bonnes nouvelles, which literally means "the good news" and refers to the gospel.

CHRISTMAS IN OUR HEARTS

We love Him because He first loved us.
1 JOHN 4:19 NKJV

Joy is simply love looking at its treasures.

A Christian's joy is in loving Christ and loving other people because Christ loves them; it is in doing good to others, and so having a Christmas perpetually.

It is in looking forward to that world of glory where we shall be like him, and shall see him as he is. "Where I am," is a sweet assurance, "ye shall be also." Jesus offers to fill our homes and our hearts with joy, if we will only let him do it.

We cannot create canary birds, but we can provide cages and food for them, and fill our dwellings with music. Even so we cannot create the spiritual gifts and blessings which the Christian Jesus offers; but they are ours if we provide heart room for them.

The birds of peace and praise and joy will fly in fast enough if we only set the doors and windows of our soul wide open for the Joy-Bringing Christ.

T. L. CUYLER

Christmas Around the World

ITALY

The Christmas season in Italy lasts three weeks. Children go from house to house reciting Christmas poems and singing. In the week before Christmas, children dress up as shepherds and walk through their neighborhoods playing pipes, singing, and reciting Christmas poems. They are given money to buy presents.

A strict fast is observed for twenty-four hours before Christmas Eve and is followed by a celebration meal. Presents or empty boxes are drawn from the Urn of Fate. By twilight, candles are lighted, prayers are said, and children recite poems.

At noon on Christmas Day, the pope gives his blessing to crowds of onlookers.

In Italy the children wait until Epiphany, January 6, for their presents. According to tradition, the presents are delivered by a kind, ugly witch named Befana. Legend has it that she was told by the Magi that the Baby Jesus was born, but she was busy and delayed visiting the baby. She missed the star over Bethlehem, lost her way, and has been flying around ever since, leaving presents at every house with children in case the Baby Jesus is there. She slides down chimneys and fills stockings and shoes with good things for good children and coal for bad children.

THE OTHER WISEMAN

HENRY VAN DYKE, 1902

On the night that the sign was to be given, Artaban was speaking to nine of his Magi friends in his home. He said to them, "My three brethren are watching at the ancient temple of the Seven Spheres, at Borsippa, in Babylon and I am watching here. If the star appears, they will wait for me (for) ten days, then we will all set out together for Jerusalem. I believe the sign will come tonight. I have made ready for the journey by selling all of my possessions and have bought these three jewels: a sapphire, a ruby, and a pearl. I intend to present them as my tribute to the King." He said, "I invite you to make the pilgrimage with us that we may worship the new-born King together."

While he was speaking he thrust his hand into the inmost fold of his girdle and drew out three (great) gems: one blue as a fragment of the night sky, one redder than a ray of the sunrise, and one as pure as the peak of a snow mountain at twilight. He would give them all to the King. Then one of Artaban's friends said, "Artaban, this is a vain dream. No King will ever rise from the broken race of Israel. He who looks for him is a chaser of shadows." Then he bid Artaban farewell and left his dwelling.

Each in turn offered his own particular excuse, and finally only his oldest and truest friend remained. He said, "Artaban, I am too old for this quest, but my heart goes with thee." Then with a hand on Artaban's shoulder he said, "Those who would see wonderful things must often be willing to travel alone."

Left to himself Artaban put his jewels back into his girdle. Then he parted the curtains and went out onto the roof to again take up his vigil to watch the night sky.

As Jupiter and Saturn rolled together like drops of lambent flame about to blend into one, an azure spark was born out of the darkness beneath them, rounding itself with purple splendor into a crimson sphere.

Artaban bowed his head. "It is the sign," he said. "The King is coming, and I will go to meet him."

All night long, Vasda, the swiftest of Artaban's horses, had been waiting saddled and bridled, in her stall, pawing the ground impatiently and shaking her bit as if she shared the eagerness of her master's purpose.

As Artaban placed himself upon her back he said, "God bless us both, and keep our feet from falling and our souls from death."

Under this encouragement, each day his faithful horse measured off the allotted proportion of the distance, and at nightfall of the tenth day, they approached the outskirts of Babylon. In a little island of desert palm trees Vasda scented difficulty and slackened her pace. Then she gave a quick breath of anxiety and stood stock-still quivering in every muscle.

Artaban dismounted. The dim starlight revealed the form of a man lying in the roadway. His humble dress and haggard face showed him to be one of the poor Hebrew exiles who still dwelt in Babylon. His pallid skin bore the mark of the deadly fever that ravished the marshlands of Babylon at this season of the year. The chill of death was in his lean hand. Artaban turned to go, a sigh came from the sick man's lips, and the brown bony fingers closed convulsively upon the Magician's robe.

Artaban felt sorry that he could not stay to minister to this dying stranger, but this was the hour toward which his entire life had been directed. He could not forfeit the reward of his years of study and faith to do a single deed of human mercy. But then, how could he leave his fellow man alone to die?

"God of truth and mercy," prayed Artaban, "direct me in the holy path of wisdom which only thou knowest." Then he knew that he could not go on. The Magicians were physicians as well as astronomers. He took off his robe and began his work of healing. Several hours later the patient regained consciousness.

Then Artaban gave him all he had left of his bread and wine. He left a potion of healing herbs and instructions for his care.

TRIVIA

The actual gift givers are different in various countries:
England: Father Christmas
France: Pere Noel (Father Christmas)
Germany: Christkind (angelic messenger from Jesus). She is a
beautiful fair-haired girl with a shining crown of candles.
Holland: St. Nicholas
Italy: La Befana (a kindly old witch)
Spain and South America: The Three Kings
Russia: In some parts of Russia, Bahouschka (a grand
motherly figure) brings the gifts; in other parts of Russia the gifts
come from Grandfather Frost.
Scandinavia: A variety of Christmas gnomes, one of whom is called
Julenisse.

Though Artaban rode with the greatest haste the rest of the way, it was after dawn that he arrived at the designated meeting place. His friends were nowhere to be seen. Finally his eyes caught a piece of parchment arranged to attract his attention. He caught it up and read.

It said, "We have waited till past the midnight, and can delay no longer. We go to find the King. Follow us across the desert."

Artaban sat down upon the ground in despair and covered his face with his hands. "How can I cross the desert with no food and with a spent horse? I must return to Babylon, sell my sapphire, and buy a train of camels and provisions for the journey. I may never overtake my friends. Only God the merciful knows whether or not I shall lose my purpose because I tarried to show mercy."

Several days later when Artaban's train arrived at Bethlehem the streets were deserted. It was rumored that Herod was sending soldiers, presumably to enforce some new tax, and the men had taken their flocks and herds back into the hills beyond his reach.

The door of one dwelling was open, and Artaban could hear a mother singing a lullaby to her child. He entered and introduced himself. The woman told him that it was now the third day since the three wise men had appeared in Bethlehem. They had found Joseph and Mary and the young child, and had laid their gifts at his feet. Then they had disappeared as mysteriously as they had come.

Joseph had taken his wife and babe that same night and had secretly fled. It was whispered that they were going far away, into Egypt.

As Artaban listened, the baby reached up its dimpled hand and touched his cheek and smiled. His heart warmed at the touch. Then suddenly outside there arose a wild confusion of sounds. Women were shrieking. Then a desperate cry said, "The soldiers of Herod are killing the children."

Artaban went to the doorway. A band of soldiers came hurrying down the street with dripping swords and bloody hands. The captain approached the door to thrust Artaban aside, but Artaban did not stir. His face was as calm as though he were still watching the stars. Finally his outstretched hand revealed the giant ruby. He said, "I am waiting to give this jewel to the prudent captain who will go on his way and leave this house alone." The captain amazed at the splendor of the gem, took it and said to his men, "March on. there are no children here."

Then Artaban prayed, "Oh, God, forgive me my sin, I have spent for men that which was meant for God. Shall I ever be worthy to see the face of the King?"

But the voice of the woman, weeping for joy in the shadows behind him said softly, "Because thou hast saved the life of my little one may the Lord bless thee and keep thee, the Lord make His face to shine upon thee and be gracious unto thee; the Lord lift up His countenance upon thee and give thee peace."

Then Artaban, still following the King, went on into Egypt, seeking everywhere for traces of the little family that had fled before him from Bethlehem. For many years we follow Artaban in his search.

We see him at the pyramids. We see him in an obscure house in Alexandria, taking counsel with a Hebrew rabbi who told him to seek the King not among the rich but among the poor. Then we follow him from place to place. He passed through countries where famine lay heavy upon the land, and the poor were crying for bread. He made his dwelling in plague-stricken cities where the sick were languishing in the bitter companionship of helpless misery. He visited the oppressed and the afflicted in the gloom of subterranean prisons. He searched the crowded wretchedness of slave-markets. Though he found no one to worship, he found many to serve. As the years passed he fed the hungry, clothed the naked, healed the sick and comforted the captive.

Once we see Artaban for a moment as he stood alone at sunrise, waiting at the gate of a Roman prison. He had taken from its secret resting place in his bosom, the last of the jewels that he was saving for the King. Shifting gleams of azure and rose trembled upon its surface. It seemed to have absorbed some of the colors of the lost sapphire and ruby; just as a noble life draws into itself its profound purpose; so that all that has helped it is transfused into its very essence, so the pearl had become more precious because it had long been carried close to the warmth of a beating human heart.

Thirty-three years had now passed away since Artaban began his search, and he was still a pilgrim. His hair was now white as snow. He knew his life's end was near, but he was still desperate with hope that he would find the king. He had come for the last time to Jerusalem.

It was the season of the Passover, and the city was thronged with strangers. There was a singular agitation visible in the multitude. A secret human tide was sweeping them toward the Damascus gate.

Artaban inquired where they were going. One answered, "We are going to the execution on Golgotha, outside the city walls. Two robbers are to be crucified, and with them another called Jesus of Nazareth, a man who has done many wonderful works among the people. But the priests and elders have said that he must die, because he claims to be the Son of God. Pilate sent him to the cross, because he said that he was the 'King of the Jews.'"

How strangely these familiar words fell upon the tired heart of Artaban. They had led him for a lifetime over land and sea. And now they came to him darkly and mysteriously like a message of despair. The King had been denied and cast out. He was now about to perish. Perhaps he was already dying. Could he be the same for whom the star had appeared thirty-three long years ago?

Artaban's heart beat loudly within him. He thought, "The ways of God are stranger than the thoughts of men, and it may be that I shall yet find the King, and be able to ransom him from death by giving my treasure to his enemies."

But as Artaban started toward Calvary he saw a troop of Macedonian soldiers coming down the street, dragging a sobbing young woman with torn dress and disheveled hair. As Artaban paused, she broke away from her tormentors and threw herself at his feet, her arms clasping around his knees.

"Have pity on me," she cried, "and save me, for the sake of the God of purity. My father was also of the Magi, but he is dead, and I am to be sold as a slave to pay his debts."

Artaban trembled as he again felt the old conflict arising in his soul. It was the same that he had experienced in the palm grove of Babylon and in the cottage at Bethlehem. Twice the gift which he had consecrated to the King had been drawn from his hand to the service of humanity. Would he now fail again? One thing was clear, he must rescue this helpless child from evil.

FACTOIDS

*Mistletoe, a traditional Christmas Symbol, was once
revered by the early Britons. It was so sacred that it had
to be cut with a golden sickle.*

He took the pearl from his bosom. Never had it seemed so luminous, so radiant, so full of tender, living luster. He laid it in the hand of the slave and said, "Daughter, this is the ransom. It is the last of my treasures which I had hoped to keep for the King."

While he yet spoke, the darkness of the sky thickened, and the shuddering tremors of an earthquake ran through the ground.

The houses rocked. The soldiers fled in terror. Artaban sank beside a protecting wall. What had he to fear? What had he to hope for? He had given away the last remnant of his tribute to the King.

The quest was over, and he had failed. What else mattered? As one lingering pulsation of the earthquake quivered beneath him, a heavy tile, shaken from the roof, fell and struck him on the temple. He lay breathless and pale. The rescued girl leaned over him fearing that he was dead. Then there came a still, small voice through the twilight. It was like distant music. The notes were clear, but the girl could not understand the words.

Then the lips of Artaban began to move, as if in answer, and she heard him say, "Not so, my Lord; for when saw I thee hungered and fed thee? Or thirsty, and gave thee drink? When saw I thee a stranger and took thee in? Or naked, and clothed thee? When saw I thee sick or in prison, and came unto thee? Thirty-three years have I looked for thee; but I have never seen thy face, nor ministered unto thee, my King."

As he ceased, the sweet voice came again. And again the maid heard it, very faintly and far away. But now she understood the words which said, "Verily, I say unto thee, that inasmuch as thou hast done it unto one of the least of these my brethren, thou hast done it unto me."

A NATIVITY PRAYER

Dear friends, we should love each other,
because love comes from God.
1 JOHN 4:7 NCV

This season can be overpowering, Lord. Sweetness and antiquity have come together again to celebrate something old and beautiful in the blood. Let us not be lost in our distractions. Let us celebrate our true nativity. Let us remember the pain that labored us here, that made us children of the Most High, love that imposed itself upon a young maiden, love that grew in her till she cried out in a night that gave Christ to the world. O, let heaven rest in me, even as it did on that cradled and quiet night so long ago, when her prince was given to us. In Jesus, my true nativity, amen.

May the wise man in you find his star. May it sparkle
in your skies like a bright jewel you cannot ignore or
lose in your distractions. May it lead you to the
Bethlehem of your latter nativity, the womb of life that
will offer you to an ungospelled world, that will set
another lover, another lamb adrift in a world of the
loveless and unsure.
DAVID TEEMS

FOOD TRADITIONS

RUSSIA

Christmas Eve dinner is meatless but festive. The most important ingredient is a special porridge called kutya. It is made of wheatberries or other grains that symbolize hope and immortality and honey and poppyseeds which ensure happiness, success, and untroubled rest. A ceremony involving the blessing of the home is frequently observed. The kutya is eaten from a common dish to symbolize unity.

The twelve foods:
1. *Mushroom soup with zaprashka; this is often replaced with sauerkraut soup*
2. *Lenten bread (pagach)*
3. *Grated garlic*
4. *Bowl of honey*
5. *Baked cod*
6. *Fresh apricots, oranges, figs, and dates*
7. *Nuts*
8. *Kidney beans (slow cooked all day) seasoned with shredded potatoes, lots of garlic, and salt and pepper to taste*
9. *Peas*
10. *Parsley potatoes (boiled new potatoes with chopped parsley and margarine)*
11. *Bobal'ki (small biscuits combined with sauerkraut or poppyseed with honey)*
12. *Red wine*

Kutya

INGREDIENTS:

2 cups wheat kernels
3 quarts water
1 cup poppy seeds
1/2 cup chopped walnuts
1 each apple, peeled, cubed 1/4 inch
1/2 cup honey
1 cup sugar

DIRECTIONS:

Dry wheat in 250° F oven for 1 hour, stirring occasionally. Rinse and soak overnight in cold water. Dissolve honey in 3/4 cup very hot water. Bring wheat to a boil, simmer for 3 to 4 hours, until the wheat kernels burst. Simmer poppy seeds for 3 to 5 minutes, drain, grind in mortar with pestle, and set aside. After ingredients are cool, combine in a bowl and add the chopped apples. Serve chilled as this will not keep well at room temperature. Store in refrigerator for up to 2 days if needed.

OPTIONS:

You may add raisins (1/3 cup), chopped dried peaches (1/3 cup), or other dried fruit, such as dried chopped cherries (1/3 cup).
Makes 6 servings.

THE DAY AFTER CHRISTMAS

Glory to God in the highest, and on earth peace,
goodwill toward men!
LUKE 2:14 NKJV

Lord, redeem us in this declining time. Exhausted, spent, the bright
season begins to steal slowly away and with its own mysterious
burden on its back, taking from us perhaps as much as it brought. The
spell is over. Call quiet upon us. Gather us to yourself before winter
blasts in our faces, before we burrow beneath our surfaces, before
lonely has a chance to brood among us once again. Let your
assurances preserve us. Let love warm us ever and deep within its
soft down coverings. Companion those neglected and overlooked.
Shelter the homeless and unprotected. Let blessedness rule among us.
Be gladness to us, Lord, our unending festival. For long after our
revels end, you are. Keep me.
In Christ, the day after and then some, amen.

May anticipation of him give the day back its color.
May it bring pinkness to the cheeks, celebration to the
heart, and thanksgiving to the tongue.

CHRISTMAS CRAFTS AND HOMEMADE GIFTS

PRACTICAL AND MOST APPRECIATED GIFTS

For Teachers

1. Non-personal items. Instead of individual gifts, consider a contribution to the class or school library.
2. School supplies. Many teachers purchase supplies with their own money for their classroom and appreciate the thought of construction paper, paints, Play-Doh, crayons, pencils, scissors, stickers, chalk, dry erase markers, or Kleenex.
3. Gift certificate to coffee shops or bakeries.
4. Thank-you notes or letters expressing appreciation for the relationship between the child and the teacher.
5. Gift certificate to a bookstore.
6. Movie gift certificate from a theater or a video/DVD rental store.
7. Gift certificate to a teacher's supply store.
8. TIME—check with the principal and then offer to supervise the classroom for an hour or two a week.

For Neighbors and Friends

1.   A plate with traditional assorted goodies. Often older couples don't bake but enjoy homemade treats for the holidays.

2.   An offer of assistance. Consider a group effort from those in the neighborhood: painting a house, mowing the yard, raking leaves, and clearing snow from sidewalks — all are wonderful gifts.

3.   Note of appreciation. Take the time to write those who have given into your life throughout the year.

4.   Cold weather bucket. Fill it with windshield deicer, lock deicer, a snow brush with a scraper on the end, a stadium blanket to keep in the car, and a thermal travel mug for coffee.

THE GEESE IN THE STORM

*For God so loved the world that he gave his one and
only Son, that whoever believes in him shall not perish
but have eternal life.*
JOHN 3:16

There was once a man who didn't believe in God, and he didn't
hesitate to let others know how he felt about religion and religious
holidays, like Christmas. His wife, however, did believe, and she
raised their children to also have faith in God and Jesus despite his
disparaging comments.

One snowy Christmas Eve, his wife was taking their children to a
Christmas Eve service in the farm community in which they lived.
She asked him to come, but he refused.

"That story is nonsense!" he said. "Why would God lower
Himself to come to Earth as a man? That's ridiculous!"

So she and the children left, and he stayed home.

A while later, the winds grew stronger and the snow turned into a
blizzard. As the man looked out the window, all he saw was a
blinding snowstorm. He sat down to relax before the fire for the
evening.

Then he heard a loud thump. Something had hit the window.
Then another thump. He looked out but couldn't see more than a few
feet. When the snow let up a little, he ventured outside to see what
could have been beating on his window. In the field near his house he
saw a flock of wild geese.

Apparently they had been flying south for the winter when they
got caught in the snowstorm and couldn't go on. They were lost and

stranded on his farm, with no food or shelter. They just flapped their wings and flew around the field in low circles, blindly and aimlessly. A couple of them had flown into his window, it seemed.

The man felt sorry for the geese and wanted to help them. The barn would be a great place for them to stay, he thought. It's warm and safe; surely they could spend the night and wait out the storm. So he walked over to the barn and opened the doors wide, then watched and waited, hoping they would notice the open barn and go inside. But the geese just fluttered around aimlessly and didn't seem to notice the barn or realize what it could mean for them.

The man tried to get their attention, but that just seemed to scare them and they moved further away.

He went into the house and came with some bread, broke it up, and made a breadcrumb trail leading to the barn. They still didn't catch on.

Now he was getting frustrated. He got behind them and tried to shoo them toward the barn, but they only got more scared and scattered in every direction except toward the barn. Nothing he did could get them to go into the barn where they would be warm and safe.

"Why don't they follow me?!" he exclaimed. "Can't they see this is the only place where they can survive the storm?"

He thought for a moment and realized that they just wouldn't follow a human. "If only I were a goose, then I could save them," he said out loud.

Then he had an idea. He went into barn, got one of his own geese, and carried it in his arms as he circled around behind the flock of wild geese. He then released it. His goose flew through the flock and straight into the barn—and one by one the other geese followed it to safety.

He stood silently for a moment as the words he had spoken a few minutes earlier replayed in his mind: "If only I were a goose, then I could save them!" Then he thought about what he had said to his wife earlier. "Why would God want to be like us? That's ridiculous!"

Suddenly it all made sense. That is what God had done. We were like the geese—blind, lost, perishing. God had His Son become like us so He could show us the way and save us. That was the meaning of Christmas, he realized.

As the winds and blinding snow died down, his soul became quiet and pondered this wonderful thought. Suddenly he understood what Christmas was all about, why Christ had come.

Years of doubt and disbelief vanished like the passing storm. He fell to his knees in the snow, and prayed his first prayer: "Thank You, God, for coming in human form to get me out of the storm!"

"Geese in the Storm'" is a slight modification of the classic written by Louis Cassels in 1959 called, "The Parable of the Birds." Cassels was United Press International senior editor and religion columnist.

TRIVIA

One notable medieval English Christmas celebration featured a giant 165-pound pie. The giant pie was nine feet in diameter. Its ingredients included two bushels of flour, twenty pounds of butter, four geese, two rabbits, four wild ducks, two woodcocks, six snipes, four partridges, two neats' tongues, two curlews, six pigeons, and seven blackbirds.

Christmas Around the World

MEXICO

Mexicans start celebrating Christmas on December 16. Nativity scenes are very common. This is a time of grand celebration and gathering. Many people take part in a reenactment of the birth of Christ. Many also attend *pastorelas* or plays about the shepherds and their visit from the angels Children will get a visit from Saint Nicholas, but many have another special Christmas spirit who brings gifts and joy. On Christmas Eve, kids can expect a visit from el Nino Dios. The Holy Child brings gifts to the good girls and boys. On January 6, the three wise men come to visit for Reyes Magos. The Magi leave more gifts for the children, sometimes in their shoes.

Mexican decorations also include beautiful red poinsettias, or *La Flor de Noche Buena*. The flower is named for Dr. Joel R. Poinsett, the American minister to Mexico in the early 1800s. A well-dressed Mexican Christmas home would also have a pinata. Because Christmas trees have to travel a great distance to Mexico, full-sized trees are expensive and usually only found in the homes of the wealthy. Other people find ways to honor the evergreen by adding ornaments to a small branch or shrub.

Many Mexican families attend a midnight mass on Christmas Eve. The birth of Christ is very much the central theme to the Mexican celebration.

LONG WALK

*And the angel said unto them, Fear not: for behold, I
bring you good tidings of great joy, which shall be to all
people.*
L U K E   2 : 1 0   K J V

The African boy listened carefully as the teacher explained why it is that Christians give presents to each other on Christmas Day. "The gift is an expression of our joy over the birth of Jesus and our friendship for each other," she said.

When Christmas Day came, the boy brought the teacher a sea shell of lustrous beauty. "Where did you ever find such a beautiful shell?" the teacher asked as she gently fingered the gift.

The youth told her that there was only one spot where such extraordinary shells could be found. When he named the place, a certain bay several miles away, the teacher was left speechless.

"Why . . . why, it's gorgeous . . . wonderful, but you shouldn't have gone all that way to get a gift for me."

His eyes brightening, the boy answered, "Long walk part of gift."

FACTOIDS
*Jesus Christ, son of Mary, was born in a cave, not in a
wooden stable. Caves were used to house animals
because of intense heat.*

FIRST BREATH

All things were created through Him and for Him.
COLOSSIANS 1:16 NKJV

The marvel of Christmas is that the Maker of the mountains took his first breath as a baby. The One who framed the universe assumed human flesh so he could save us. The incarnation is the astounding combination of who descended from heaven to earth, how he arrived, and why he came. "For by Him all things were created . . . And He is before all things, and in Him all things consist . . . For it pleased the Father that in Him all the fullness should dwell, and by Him to reconcile all things to Himself, . . . having made peace through the blood of His cross" (Col. 1:16-20 NKJV).

When Jesus took his first breath on earth, a loving promise of God the Father was fulfilled. The Christ child whom the angels announced and the shepherds proclaimed had come to die.

The baby in the manger was "the image of the invisible God, the firstborn over all creation" (v. 15), "in whom we have redemption through His blood, the forgiveness of sins" (v. 14). The tiny baby in the manger is the mighty Creator of the universe.

TRIVIA

In Victorian England, turkeys were popular for Christmas dinners. Some of the birds were raised in Norfolk and taken to market in London. To get them to London, the turkeys were supplied with boots made of sacking or leather. The turkeys were walked to market. The boots protected their feet from the frozen mud of the road. Boots were not used for geese; instead, their feet were protected with a covering of tar.

THE MIRACULOUS STAIRCASE

ARTHUR GORDON

On that cool December morning in 1878, sunlight lay like an amber rug across the dusty streets and adobe houses of Santa Fe. It glinted on the bright tile roof of the almost completed Chapel of Our Lady of Light and on the nearby windows of the convent school run by the Sisters of Loretto. Inside the convent the Mother Superior looked up from her packing as a tap came on her door.

"It's another carpenter, Reverend Mother," said Sister Francis Louise, her round face apologetic. "I told him that you're leaving right away, that you haven't time to see him, but he says . . ."

"I know what he says," Mother Magdalene said, going on resolutely with her packing. "That he's heard about our problem with the new chapel. That he's the best carpenter in all of New Mexico. That he can build us a staircase to the choir loft despite the fact that the brilliant architect in Paris who drew the plans failed to leave any space for one. And despite the fact that five master carpenters have already tried and failed. You're quite right, Sister; I don't have time to listen to that story again."

FACTOID

In 1947, Toys for Tots started making the holidays a little happier for children by organizing its first Christmas toy drive for needy youngsters.

"But he seems like such a nice man," said Sister Francis Louise wistfully, "and he's out there with his burro, and . . ."

"I'm sure," said Mother Magdalene with a smile, "that he's a charming man, and that his burro is a charming donkey. But there's sickness down at the Santo Domingo pueblo, and it may be cholera. Sister Mary Helen and I are the only ones here who've had cholera. So we have to go. And you have to stay and run the school. And that's that!" Then she called, "Manuela!"

A young Indian girl of twelve or thirteen, black haired and smiling, came in quietly on moccasined feet. She was a mute. She could hear and understand, but the Sisters had been unable to teach her to speak. The Mother Superior spoke to her gently: "Take my things down to the wagon, child. I'll be right there." And to Sister Francis Louise: "You'd better tell your carpenter friend to come back in two or three weeks. I'll see him then."

"Two or three weeks! Surely you'll be home for Christmas?"

"If it's the Lord's will, Sister, I hope so."

FACTOIDS
In 1937, the first postage stamp to commemorate Christmas was issued in Austria.

In the street, beyond the waiting wagon, Mother Magdalene could see the carpenter, a bearded man, strongly built and taller than most Mexicans, with dark eyes and a smiling, wind-burned face. Beside him, laden with tools and scraps of lumber, a small gray burro stood patiently. Manuela was stroking its nose, glancing shyly at its owner. "You'd better explain," said the Mother Superior, "that the child can hear him, but she can't speak."

Good-byes were quick — the best kind when you leave a place you love. Southwest, then along the dusty trail, the mountains purple with shadow, the Rio Grande a ribbon of green far off to the right. The pace was slow, but Mother Magdalene and Sister Mary Helen amused themselves by singing songs and telling Christmas stories as the sun marched up and down the sky. And their leathery driver listened and nodded.

Two days of this brought them to Santo Domingo pueblo, where the sickness was not cholera after all, but measles, almost as deadly in an Indian village. And so they stayed, helping the harassed Father Sebastian, visiting the dark adobe hovels where feverish brown children tossed and fierce Indian dogs showed their teeth.

TRIVIA

In Greek legend, malicious creatures called kallikantzaroi (also spelled kallikantzari) sometimes play troublesome pranks at Christmas time. According to the legend, to get rid of them, you should burn either salt or an old shoe. Apparently the stench of the burning shoe (or salt) drives off the kallikantzaroi. Other effective methods include banging a pig's jawbone by the door and keeping a large fire so they can't sneak down the chimney.

At night they were bone-weary, but sometimes Mother Magdalene found time to talk to Father Sebastian about her plans for the dedication of the new chapel. It was to be in April; the Archbishop himself would be there. And it might have been dedicated sooner, were it not for this incredible business of a choir loft with no means of access — unless it were a ladder.

"I told the Bishop," said Mother Magdalene, "that it would be a mistake to have the plans drawn in Paris. If something went wrong, what could we do? But he wanted our chapel in Santa Fe patterned after the Sainte Chapelle in Paris, and who am I to argue with Bishop Lamy? So the talented Monsieur Mouly designs a beautiful choir loft high up under the rose window, and no way to get to it."

"Perhaps," sighed Father Sebastian, "he had in mind a heavenly choir. The kind with wings."

"It's not funny," said Mother Magdalene a bit sharply. "I've prayed and prayed, but apparently there's no solution at all. There just isn't room on the chapel floor for the supports such a staircase needs."

The days passed, and with each one Christmas drew closer. Twice, horsemen on their way from Santa Fe to Albuquerque brought letters from Sister Francis Louise. All was well at the convent, but Mother Magdalene frowned over certain paragraphs. "The children are getting ready for Christmas," Sister Francis Louise wrote in her first letter. "Our little Manuela and the carpenter have become great friends. It's amazing how much he seems to know about us all . . ."

And what, thought Mother Magdalene, is the carpenter still doing there? The second letter also mentioned the carpenter.

"Early every morning he comes with another load of lumber, and every night he goes away. When we ask him by what authority he does these things, he smiles and says nothing. We have tried to pay him for his work, but he will accept no pay . . ."

FACTOID

In medieval England, Nicholas was just another saint - he has not yet been referred to as Santa Claus, and he had nothing to do with Christmas.

Work? What work? Mother Magdalene wrinkled up her nose in exasperation. Had that softhearted Sister Francis Louise given the man permission to putter around in the new chapel? With firm and disapproving hand, the Mother Superior wrote a note ordering an end to all such unauthorized activities. She gave it to an Indian pottery-maker on his way to Santa Fe.

But that night the first snow fell, so thick and heavy that the Indian turned back. Next day at noon the sun shone again on a world glittering with diamonds. But Mother Magdalene knew that another snowfall might make it impossible for her to be home for Christmas.

By now the sickness at Santo Domingo was subsiding. And so that afternoon they began the long ride back.

The snow did come again, making their slow progress even slower. It was late on Christmas Eve, close to midnight, when the tired horses plodded up to the convent door. But lamps still burned. Manuela flew down the steps, Sister Francis Louise close behind her. And chilled and weary though she was,

Mother Magdalene sensed instantly an excitement, an electricity in the air that she could not understand. Nor did she understand it when they led her, still in her heavy wraps, down the corridor into the new, as yet unused chapel, where a few candles burned. "Look, Reverend Mother," breathed Sister Francis Louise. "Look!"

Like a curl of smoke the staircase rose before them, as insubstantial as a dream. Its base was on the chapel floor; its top rested against the choir loft. Nothing else supported it; it seemed to float on air. There were no banisters. Two complete spirals it made, the polished wood gleaming softly in the candlelight.

TRIVIA

Myrrh is an aromatic gum resin which oozes from gashes cut in the bark of a small desert tree known as Commifera Myrrh or the dindin tree. The myrrh hardens into tear-dropped shaped chunks and is then powdered or made into ointments or perfumes. This tree is about five to fifteen feet tall and one foot in diameter. Legend says that Caspar brought the gift of myrrh from Europe or Tarsus and placed it before the Christ Child. Myrrh was an extremely valuable commodity during biblical times and was imported from India and Arabia.

"Thirty-three steps," whispered Sister Francis Louise. "One for each year in the life of Our Lord."

Mother Magdalene moved forward like a woman in a trance. She put her foot on the first step, then the second, then the third.

There was no tremor.

She looked down, bewildered, at Manuela's ecstatic, upturned face. "But it's impossible! There wasn't time!"

"He finished yesterday," the Sister said. "He didn't come today. No one has seen him anywhere in Santa Fe. He's gone.

"But who was he? Don't you even know his name?"

The Sister shook her head, but now Manuela pushed forward, nodding emphatically. Her mouth opened; she took a deep, shuddering breath; she made a sound that was like a gasp in the stillness. The nuns stared at her, transfixed. She tried again. This time it was a syllable, followed by another. "Jo-se." She clutched the Mother Superior's arm and repeated the first word she had ever spoken. "Jose!"

Sister Francis Louise crossed herself. Mother Magdalene felt her heart contract. Jose—the Spanish word for Joseph. Joseph the Carpenter. Joseph the Master Woodworker of . . .

"Jose!" Manuela's dark eyes were full of tears. "Jose!" Silence, then, in the shadowy chapel. No one moved. Far away across the snow-silvered town Mother Magdalene heard a bell tolling midnight. She came down the stairs and took Manuela's hand. She felt uplifted by a great surge of wonder and gratitude and compassion and love. And she knew what it was. It was the spirit of Christmas.

And it was upon them all.

FOR FUN

TOP 10 WORST GIFTS TO GIVE YOUR BOSS

10. Fruitcake, any flavor
9. Leadership for Dummies
8. A gift certificate for a resume-writing service
7. A pound of decaf coffee
6. Tickets to "War and Peace on Ice"
5. A copy of Lead Like Ebenezer: Giving Scrooge a Run for His Money
4. A Bible with passages underlined about treating employees fairly
3. A Dilbert mug
2. Close-ups of you and the staff taken on the company photocopier
1. Two weeks' notice

AUTHOR'S NOTE:

The wonderful thing about legends is the way they grow. Through the years they can be told and retold and embroidered a bit more each time. This, indeed, is such a retelling.

But all good legends contain a grain of truth, and in this case the irrefutable fact at the heart of the legend is the inexplicable staircase itself.

You may see it yourself in Santa Fe today. It stands just as it stood when the chapel was dedicated almost ninety years ago— except for the banister, which was added later. Tourists stare and marvel. Architects shake their heads and murmur, "Impossible." No one knows the identity of the designer-builder. All the Sisters know is that the problem existed, a stranger came, solved it, and left.

The thirty-three steps make two complete turns without central support. There are no nails in the staircase; only wooden pegs. The curved stringers are put together with exquisite precision; the wood is spliced in seven places on the inside and nine on the outside. The wood is said to be a hard-fir variety, nonexistent in New Mexico. School accounts show no record that any payment for the staircase was ever made.

Home for Christmas: Stories for the Young and Old, compiled by Miriam Leblanc, © 2002. The Plough Publishing Foundation of the Bruderhof Foundation. Inc., published 2004. Orbis Books Maryknoll, NY 10545-0308

FOOD TRADITIONS

RUSSIA

Lenten Bread (Pagach)

INGREDIENTS:

2.5 cups flour
1 cup warm water
1 package yeast
1/2 teaspoon salt
1 large onion peeled and sliced
1 medium head of cabbage, shredded
1/2 cup oil
salt
pepper

DIRECTIONS:

Dissolve yeast in water, add salt and flour, and knead until smooth and elastic, adding more flour as needed. Place dough on countertop and cover with a stainless-steel bowl. Allow to rise double in bulk.

Sauté onion in oil until soft. Add shredded cabbage and salt and pepper and cover and cook until cabbage is tender and soft. Drain off any excess oil. Punch down dough and divide into 2 parts.

Roll out dough into an 18 x 12-inch rectangle. Place cooled filling on one side of rectangle, leaving a 2-inch margin from the edges. Fold the other half of dough over the filling so you have a turnover, 9 x 12 inches. Pat the top of the dough down lightly on the filling.

Carefully pinch edges together. Brush oil over the top of the dough and sprinkle with salt or garlic salt. Place on greased baking sheet. Let rise double.

Bake at 400° F for 30 minutes or until golden brown.

Christmas Around the World

SWITZERLAND

A tinkling of a silver bell heralds the arrival of *Christkindli*, a white-clad angel with a face veil held in place by a jeweled crown. The tree candles are lit as she enters each house and hands out presents from the basket held by her child helpers.

Bell ringing has become a tradition, and each village competes with the next when calling people to midnight mass.

After the service, families gather to share huge homemade doughnuts, called *Ringli*, and hot chocolate.

During the holiday season, star singers or *Sternsingers* dressed as the Magi parade through the streets of cities and towns singing Christmas songs. In Zurich, Santa visits in a special fairy-tale tram and gives the children a ride through the city, singing songs and sharing a basket full of sweets.

FOR FUN

CHECKLIST FOR A BETTER YEAR

- ☐ *Read through the Bible.*
- ☐ *Be an encourager.*
- ☐ *Play with the kids at least three times each week.*
- ☐ *Exercise twenty-five minutes or more four days each week.*
- ☐ *Rekindle the romance.*
- ☐ *Eat more veggies.*
- ☐ *Spend less.*
- ☐ *Save more.*
- ☐ *Take initiative to build a friendship.*
- ☐ *Listen, don't lecture.*
- ☐ *Look for the blessings.*
- ☐ *Pray more.*
- ☐ *Laugh more.*
- ☐ *Trust God more.*
- ☐ *Relax more.*

OUR CHRISTMAS MEMORIES AND TRADITIONS

A MEMORABLE YEAR _____

MEMORIES OF THE PAST YEAR

_____

_____

_____

_____

_____

_____

_____

_____

_____

_____

WE GATHERED FOR THE HOLIDAYS AT

_____

_____

_____

_____

TRADITIONS AND SPECIAL EVENTS

_____
_____
_____
_____
_____
_____
_____
_____
_____
_____
_____
_____
_____
_____
_____
_____

THOSE WHO JOINED IN THE CELEBRATIONS

_____
_____
_____
_____
_____
_____
_____
_____

OUR CHRISTMAS MEMORIES AND TRADITIONS

A MEMORABLE YEAR _____

MEMORIES OF THE PAST YEAR

_____

_____

_____

_____

_____

_____

_____

_____

_____

_____

WE GATHERED FOR THE HOLIDAYS AT

_____

_____

_____

_____

TRADITIONS AND SPECIAL EVENTS

_____

_____

_____

_____

_____

_____

_____

_____

_____

_____

_____

_____

_____

_____

_____

_____

THOSE WHO JOINED IN THE CELEBRATIONS

_____

_____

_____

_____

_____

_____

_____

_____

OUR CHRISTMAS MEMORIES AND TRADITIONS

A MEMORABLE YEAR _____

MEMORIES OF THE PAST YEAR

_____
_____
_____
_____
_____
_____
_____
_____
_____
_____

WE GATHERED FOR THE HOLIDAYS AT

_____
_____
_____
_____

TRADITIONS AND SPECIAL EVENTS

_____
_____
_____
_____
_____
_____
_____
_____
_____
_____
_____
_____
_____
_____
_____

THOSE WHO JOINED IN THE CELEBRATIONS

_____
_____
_____
_____
_____
_____
_____
_____

OUR CHRISTMAS MEMORIES AND TRADITIONS

A MEMORABLE YEAR _____

MEMORIES OF THE PAST YEAR

_____

_____

_____

_____

_____

_____

_____

_____

_____

WE GATHERED FOR THE HOLIDAYS AT

_____

_____

_____

_____

TRADITIONS AND SPECIAL EVENTS

_____
_____
_____
_____
_____
_____
_____
_____
_____
_____
_____
_____
_____
_____
_____
_____
_____

THOSE WHO JOINED IN THE CELEBRATIONS

_____
_____
_____
_____
_____
_____
_____
_____

SECTION 4

The True Story of Christmas

THE TRUE STORY OF CHRISTMAS

A long, long time before Jesus was born, the Lord told a man named Isaiah that a future king was coming. The Lord told Isaiah that a virgin would conceive this child and that he would be called, "The Mighty God." God also told Isaiah that this coming king's kingdom would have no end. "Behold, a virgin shall conceive, and bear a son, and shall call his name Emmanuel. For unto us a child is born, unto us a son is given: and the government shall be upon his shoulder: and his name shall be called Wonderful, Counselor, The mighty God, The everlasting Father, The Prince of Peace. Of the increase of his government and peace there shall be no end, upon the throne of David, and upon his kingdom, to order it, and to establish it with judgment and with justice from henceforth even for ever" (Isa. 7:14; 9:6-7 KJV).

Many years after Isaiah saw the vision concerning the coming king, God sent the angel Gabriel to a virgin who lived in Nazareth, a town in Galilee. She was engaged to marry a man named Joseph from the family of David. Her name was Mary. The angel came to her and said, "Greetings! The Lord has blessed you and is with you."

But Mary was confused by what the angel said. Mary wondered, "What does this mean?"

The angel said to her, "Don't be afraid, Mary, because God is pleased with you. Listen! You will become pregnant. You will give birth to a son, and you will name him Jesus. He will be great, and people will call him the Son of the Most High. The Lord God, will give him the throne of King David, his ancestor. He will rule over the people of Jacob forever. His kingdom will never end." (Luke 1:26-33)

Mary said to the angel, "How will this happen? I am a virgin!"

The angel said to Mary, "The Holy Spirit will come upon you, and the power of the Most High will cover you. The baby will be holy. He will be called the Son of God.

Mary said, "I am the servant girl of the Lord. Let this happen to me as you say!" Then the angel went away (Luke 1:34 – 35, 38).

All of this happened to fulfill the prophecy of Isaiah many, many years earlier!

At that time, Augustus Caesar sent an order to all people in the countries that were under Roman rule. The order said that they must list their names in a register. This was the first registration taken while Quirinius was governor of Syria. And everyone went to their own towns to be registered. So Joseph left Nazareth, a town in Galilee. He went to the town of Bethlehem in Judea. This town was known as the town of David. Joseph went there because he was from the family of David. Joseph registered with Mary because she was engaged to marry him. (Mary was now pregnant.) While Joseph and Mary were in Bethlehem, the time came for her to have the baby. She gave birth to her first son. There were no rooms left in the inn so she wrapped the baby with cloths and laid him in a box where animals are fed (Luke 2:1-7).

That night, some shepherds were in the fields nearby watching their sheep. An angel of the Lord stood before them. The glory of the Lord was shining around them, and suddenly they became very frightened. The angel said to them, "Don't be afraid, because I am bringing you some good news. It will be a joy to all the people. Today your Savior was born in David's town. He is Christ, the Lord. This is how you will know him: You will find a baby wrapped in cloths and lying in a feeding box" (Luke 2:8-12).

So the shepherds went quickly and found Mary and Joseph. And the shepherds saw the baby lying in a feeding box. Then they told what the angels had said about this child. Everyone was amazed when they heard what the shepherds said to them. Mary hid these things in her heart; she continued to think about them. "Then the shepherds went back to their sheep, praising God and thanking him for everything that they had seen and heard. It was just as the angel had told them" (Luke 2:16-20).

When the baby was eight days old, he was circumcised, and he was named Jesus. This name had been given by the angel before the baby began to grow inside Mary (Luke 2:21).

Jesus was born in the town of Bethlehem in Judea during the time when Herod was king. After Jesus was born, some wise men from the east came to Jerusalem. They asked, "Where is the baby who was born to be the king of the Jews? We saw his star in the east. We came to worship him."

When King Herod heard about this new king of the Jews, he was troubled. And all the people in Jerusalem were worried too.

Herod called a meeting of all the leading priests and teachers of the law. He asked them where the Christ would be born. They answered, "In the town of Bethlehem in Judea. The prophet wrote about this in the Scriptures: 'But you, Bethlehem, in the land of Judah, you are important among the rulers of Judah. A ruler will come from you. He will be like a shepherd for my people, the Israelites'" (Mic. 5:2).

Then Herod had a secret meeting with the wise men from the east. He learned from them the exact time they first saw the star. Then Herod sent the wise men to Bethlehem. He said to them, "Go and look carefully to find the child. When you find him, come tell me. Then I can go worship him too."

The wise men heard the king and then left. They saw the same star they had seen in the east. It went before them until it stopped above the place where the child was. When the wise men saw the star, they were filled with joy. They went to the house where the child was and saw him with his mother, Mary. They bowed down and worshiped the child. They opened the gifts they brought for him. They gave him treasures of gold, frankincense, and myrrh. But God warned the wise men in a dream not to go back to Herod. So they went home to their own country by a different way.

All Scripture references are the author's paraphrase unless otherwise indicated.

SOURCES

www.santasearch.org
http://members.tripod.com/~wackyanne/library
www.allthingschristmas.com
www.online-literature.com
http://home.att.net/~quotations/christmas.html
www.quotegarden.com/christmas.html
http://quotations.about.com
www.quotelady.com
www.thehistoryofchristmas.com
www.allspirit.co.uk/christmas
www.quotedb.com
http://www.cvc.org/christmas/joy2w.htm
http://www.funandgames.org/hunt/carols.htm
www.history.uk.com
www.christmascarnivals.com
http://en.wikipedia.org
www.billpetro.com
www.whatsaiththescripture.com
www.iac.es/galeria
www.thefamily.org
http://hymnsandcarolsofchristmas.com
www.phillyburbs.com
www.catholicexchange.com
www.christmas-stories.com
http://italian.about.com
www.epicurious.com/recipes
www.whitehouse.gov

www.familycorner.com
www.betterbudgeting.com
www.christian-homemaking.com
www.dotcom.ca/holidays
www.butlerwebs.com
www.homeandholidays.com
www.rbc.org/odb
www.basicjokes.com
www.wrapcandy.com
www.suite101.com
www.familycrafts.about.com
www.holidayfamilyfun.com
www.lhj.com
www.dep.state.pa.us
www.people.cornell.edu
www.xmas-jokes.com
www.knoxvilletennessee.com
www.carols.org.uk/christmas_poem.htm
www.geocities.com/~perkinshome/story.html

www.ingramcontent.com/pod-product-compliance
Lightning Source LLC
Chambersburg PA
CBHW061133120626
46546CB00005B/1767